Purple Mums

A True Story of Surviving a Stranger Rape
And How Faith, Family, and Therapy
Guided the Road to Recovery

Sandy Madsen

PUBLISHED BY WESTVIEW, INC.
KINGSTON SPRINGS, TENNESSEE

Published by Westview, Inc.
P.O. Box 605
Kingston Springs, TN 37082
www.publishedbywestview.com

© 2013 Sandra Kay Madsen
All rights reserved, including the right to reproduction in whole or in part in any form.

ISBN 978-1-937763-96-1

First edition, May 2013

Front cover illustration by Jerry Palmer.
Back cover photograph of the author courtesy Joan McGee Photography.

Printed in the United States of America on acid free paper.

Dedicated to

The Nashville Sexual Assault Center

where they say,
"The healing starts here."

For me, it did.

FOREWORD

My wife came home on a Saturday afternoon and saw me sitting at our kitchen table crying. Since she has rarely seen me crying she immediately began thinking that someone must have died or something happened to one of our children. I told her that I had just finished reading a rough draft of a book that Sandy Madsen and her family had written, and since my wife had also met Sandy, I gave her the document to read. It was not long before my wife was also crying. I have thought often of the day and why I reacted the way I did to this book.

I have had the privilege of serving as the president of the Sexual Assault Center in Nashville, Tennessee for nineteen years, and during that time I have heard the stories of many survivors. While I know that each survivor's experience is unique to them, I also know that I have shared so many experiences with survivors that I tend to be able to handle them pretty well. What was it about Sandy's story that brought me to tears?

Sandy has told me several times that she was not the only one raped that day. The rapist raped her entire family. I understood that she did not mean that literally, but as I read this book, Sandy's words came into sharp focus for me. Sandy and her family share their personal thoughts and feelings about how this rape impacted their family. You get to read how each family member reacted and the challenges they face. You will understand what Sandy meant when she said that he raped her entire family.

I think my tears came because I have gotten to know Sandy and Dave, and their children more than most survivors who have turned to the Center for help. I have seen how remarkable this family truly is, and the unique way that they approached the writing of this book shows how a rape directly impacts the lives of more than the primary victim.

My first real memory of Sandy was the day she spoke to our board of directors. I had asked Dr. Char Creason to invite Sandy to attend our board meeting to share her experience so that our board could see how the work we do helps survivors heal. Char told me that this would be good for Sandy, and I knew it would benefit our board members. Not long after she began she had tears rolling down her face and I saw how difficult it was for her to speak about her experience.

After she finished I met her in the hallway with the intention of apologizing for asking her to share something so difficult. I was surprised that Sandy greeted me by thanking me for giving her this experience. She said that it was hard but very rewarding and that she felt great. She told me that she was doing something to help others and that was very important to her.

This was the first of many talks that Sandy has given to help others understand. I saw strength in Sandy that day that I have seen many times since. She cares so much about others that she is not going to let the horrors that she experienced as a rape victim keep her from helping others. I know that Sandy and her family have struggled tremendously to cope with the rape and its impact on each of them. But I also have seen a family that had reached out to help others.

Dave has given so much of his personal time to help other survivors. He joined the board of the Center and served on our executive committee. He has personally raised thousands of dollars to help others heal from sexual assault. Their daughters have also helped by asking others to help, resulting in the donation of a major air conditioning unit for our facility.

As you read this book you will learn how the rape of one person impacted those closest to her. You will hear their perspective of how each of them felt, and you will begin to see what a remarkable family this is. I give thanks to the entire Madsen family for once again helping others by sharing their experience.

Tim Tohill, President
Sexual Assault Center
Nashville, TN

SANDY
Purple Mums

Chapter One

Do I dare move? I think I heard the door from the laundry room close. That must mean he is gone. I'll lie here a few more seconds to be sure. Heine seems quiet now. My poor old miniature dachshund (14 years old) was so nervous, but now seemed calm. My mind was so fizzy but I did realize that I had just been brutally raped, by whom I did not have an answer.

I needed to see! I had duct tape from the top of my head to just the end of my nose. I had to free my hands first which were tied behind my back with a very tight rope. Several tugs with my arms seemed to loosen the rope enough so I could wiggle my hands free. Now I needed to pull up the duct tape above my eyes. If I tried to remove too much, all my hair would rip out. It was so tight, so I gingerly moved it back and forth until I could see.

Oh my gosh, I was so afraid to look at the surroundings. I knew I was still in the kitchen because I could feel the tile floor underneath me. I was sure he was gone and I had to lock the doors and close the garage door in case he decided to come back. I needed to call 911, check all the windows and get some clothes on and, and....I could not get a grip on what just happened but needed to make myself feel as safe as possible.

Again I realized I had just been raped by a stranger. Why?

Both eyes were finally uncovered and I needed to open them to see where I was in the room. I was between the wall and the kitchen table. I don't remember getting there as I thought I was by the dining room. I looked around and found the strength to stand acknowledging the fact I had survived something so traumatic that maybe I was just dreaming. On the other hand, I never dreamed something like this would happen to me. No, this was the real deal. I stood for a few seconds with my hands on the table as I almost passed out from weakness. My mind was finally starting to think clearly and I knew I had to get things done. Lock the doors, close the garage door, find a robe or something and call 911. You must report this right now!

I'll tell the story about the rape in detail, but the first few minutes were very important (now as I look back) in my recovery as a survivor of a stranger rape. Knowing the attack was totally NOT my fault and realizing not only had I been a victim but was a survivor. This must roll through your mind constantly or recovery will have a hard time finding a place in your life. Plus the fact you need help and support pronto. Not in a few hours, days or years but immediately.

I rapidly went around the house securing everything. I still had the duct tape on my head and had to keep pushing it up so I could see, knowing it was evidence and if there were fingerprints that could be identified later. I dialed 911 and got a busy signal. Surely not, so I tried again. After several attempts (it was discovered later that 911 lines were down for 30 minutes for the first time in the area), getting the same busy signal I gave up and called my neighbor from across the street. I didn't have the energy to look up the police station number. I told her to hurry and bring something to protect herself just in case.

I saw her walk up to the door carrying a baseball bat. God love her. I told her I had been attacked and couldn't get ahold of 911. Luckily she knew the police station number and called them immediately. It was only 4 or 5 minutes and several police cars arrived at the front of our house with a dog in tow. Not long afterwards I could hear a helicopter circling the area. She ran to the front door so they could walk right in. I sat at the kitchen table, by now shock had settled into my body. I was losing my grip and anxiety was well on its way. I'll have a chapter on the police staff, hospital staff, etc. as it is so important to be treated with respect and be respectful in return.

Chapter Two

The day of the rape had started so beautifully. It was comfortably warm and sunny for an August day in the north. It was August 31, 1994. I had worked out at the gym with some friends which I did three days a week. One of my friends was going to drive me home as I had taken my car in to be serviced. We decided to lunch at our favorite Greek restaurant, arriving home about 12:20.

The day before I had shopped at a local nursery and bought several containers of purple mums to plant around the house. We had a great home that was finished in a pinkish colored brick and I thought the purple mums would add to the beauty of the landscape. I wanted to get them in the ground before we left on Thursday for Brentwood, TN to meet with our daughters for Labor Day weekend. We had lived in Brentwood prior to our move to Dyer and our daughters had remained in the area. Our youngest daughter, Amy, had just become engaged to her longtime boyfriend, Steve. We were very happy about the engagement and were going down to celebrate and, of course, see the ring.

It was 1:00 and I needed to get myself in gear. Plant the mums, take our dog Heine to the kennel for boarding and pack for the long weekend. My husband Dave was on the road for his job as General Manager of Cargill Steel and Wire, Chicago plant. He would be home later in the evening and I wanted to be ready to leave Thursday morning.

After I had changed from my gym outfit into shorts and a lightweight sweatshirt (I remember it was pink), and with digger in hand, I got the plants out of the garage and started in the front yard. I left the garage door open (big, big mistake) as I knew I would be in and out of the garage. It didn't take long in the front yard and I started moving around the house to the side and back. We lived on a cul-de-sac and our house was actually the only house as it was a new area of the subdivision. There was a small lake on the side of the house and a small ravine to our back but we could see other houses. In front of our house was the street and across was land being readied to build more homes in the spring but the side street continued into a developed area.

I worked in the back planting the remainder of the mums. About 2:00, I knew I needed to wrap things up. I wanted to take a shower before I took Heine to the kennel.

Putting my garden tools away, I closed the garage door, walked through the laundry room taking my garden shoes off.

Walking into the kitchen I looked at the digital clock on the microwave and it read 2:03 (I will never forget that time again). Get going Sandy was on my mind. I had just reached the kitchen table when my head went to my left towards the family room. From around that corner of the wall between the kitchen and family room, came a person, MASKED!! From my quick glance I saw a dark ski –type mask, long sleeved red shirt (not tucked in), dark jeans and dark shoes, probably tennis shoe. The only flesh I noticed was white hands. First I thought it was someone surprising me, possibly a joke? But it took only a matter of a few seconds to realize this was not a joke and I needed to get to a door. I started towards the front door (I had to move through the foyer). My left hand had been on the back of a kitchen chair where I had stood frozen when I first saw the man. I would probably say in height about 5'10". That's it.

I started to run for the front door but was grabbed at the wrist of my left hand. I was at the threshold between the kitchen and foyer (This is very difficult to write). He wrapped my left arm around to my back, took his knees and buckled them to mine, knocking me to the floor. My forehead hit the ceramic tile hard making me very dizzy. Some of the next seconds are somewhat foggy but he started hitting me in the back of the head, smashing the front of my face into the floor over and over. I had my hair in a ponytail and that was a great handle for him to grab. I almost passed out from the pain but my screaming kept my oxygen flowing. The next thing I knew was duct tape being wrapped around my head. Starting at the top of my forehead and kept going to just above the nostrils. He then got up as I am sure he was getting some rope to tie me up. I wasn't going to give up easily and thought this was my chance to get to the door. I was sure I was still at the threshold and only 10' from the front door. I got up on all fours as my head by now was really pounding and I couldn't see because of the tape. As I tried to go forward I suddenly hit a wall. I also heard at this time a drawer opening, getting a knife as I realized later. All of a sudden my head was jerked back and the head beating began again, using the other hand to grab my arm. I was so very dizzy. He got my other arm before I could fight, pulled them both behind me and tied them together.

I was flipped over and he sat on my legs. I tried to kick but was so faint from the head banging that it took all my strength and my wit was leaving me fast. At that point, I felt the knife at the side of my neck and was told to stop screaming and be quiet or be dead. That is all he ever said. I heard Heine whimper as I could hear him barking and was sure he was grabbing his pant leg. He must have shoved him with his foot as Heine yipped a bit and then was quiet. I did say at that point please don't hurt my dog, he is very old.

Now the shorts and panties were being ripped off, very quickly. He tied a rope around my ankles although not very tight. He must have taken off his mask as I could feel his face. No facial hair and from what I could tell no hair on his head. The face was very smooth so he wasn't an older man. The sex part was very fast – not pleasant, in fact abusive. By this time he seemed more mean spirited. Remember, rape is all about power. So very demeaning to me as I was helpless, fogged over and yet I still wanted to fight. You hear that you shouldn't take rape personal since it is all about power, but I did and still do take it very personally. That's when the killing can come in. The ejaculation happened on my stomach so am very sure this was not his first rape. He quickly got up after kicking my legs. I wasn't able to see where he was moving, but I did hear footsteps towards the kitchen sink. Above the sink was a wide window shelf where I kept hand cream. I also heard water running. Moments later he came back with a warm cloth and ran the cloth across my stomach. I am sure he thought this would remove any semen off my skin. Then came the hand cream which he rubbed on me. I stayed extremely still not wanting to irritate him in any way. Plus I was so darn scared he would use the knife to silence me forever. Oh, the moments of not knowing were very long and I was sure I was going into shock as I was shaking uncontrollably. Fear does strange things to the body. God and family were foremost on my mind, praying and saying good-bye yet feeling some strength coming back. A knife stab must really hurt. As I was lying there, I could hear him walking around, gathering the rope, etc. Then the footsteps became distant, probably in the laundry room but I didn't know where I was in the kitchen. Then the sound of a door opening and closing quickly. I stayed still a few more seconds. I heard Heine's nails on the ceramic floor clicking towards me. It was a slow cautious sound but moving towards me. I sat up and told him I was fine. As I mentioned before I tried to be methodical in the next few minutes, all the time thanking God for sparing my life. Also thinking what an idiot I had been to leave that garage door open while I was in the back of the house. The police reported later they found footprints all around my windows. That means he was watching me the whole time I was planting following my every move from inside. Creepy thought. After checking windows, I ran back to the bedroom and put on a clean pair of panties, but did not shower or try to do anything that might be a factor in catching this horrible creature. As I walked back to the phone, I saw my clothes lying on the floor and almost threw up.

Chapter Three

The arrival of the police was so comforting. I knew I was in shock, crying and shaking so hard I could hear my teeth rattle. They came in very quietly as my neighbor, Toni, told them it was a rape but didn't know details. I don't know how many were in the house, but seemed like a lot. Much was a blur and yet so vivid, if that make any sense. They had on rubber gloves which freaked me out as the rapist also wore them.

I never moved from the chair and kept my head down. One officer got on his knees in front of me and his first question was if I was hurt and should we leave for the hospital immediately. I said no but then I could hear sirens from an ambulance. He then asked if he should remove the duct tape from my head. I said ok but please do not cut my hair. They did the best they could although I could hear my hair ripping in the back. That was of some relief. Thank goodness my hair had been in a ponytail as it probably saved most of my hair. A different policeman asked questions such as place of the attack, did I see his face (no), height, and weight, color of clothes and skin color. I told him I had only seen the rapist for a few seconds but had seen the color of his shirt, white hands, and that horrible ski mask. I told them to the best of my ability of a description. Other officers were walking around the house. They did pick up on tennis shoe markings in the carpet. Fortunately I had vacuumed the day before, so prints were easily detected. The shoe prints were at every window and door. They were also checking for finger or handprints. They did find a man's handprint on the washer, but later discovered it was Dave's print. The attacker apparently had gloves on the whole time. They bagged my clothes from the floor.

By now there was a large crowd of people standing outside, mainly across the street as the police kept them at bay. They didn't want anyone on the lawn so any foot or shoe prints would remain fresh. They took extra caution from the side door towards the small lake. The dog was everywhere sniffing. By now I was aware of a helicopter overhead. I asked if that was for me and, of course, the answer was yes.

The police asked if I would come into the dining room and look out the window. I was so amazed at all the neighbors that had gathered. There was a man standing in the crowd with a red shirt, etc. They had to help me walk as I was still weak and dizzy. I had always wondered where I got the strength to check all the doors and windows, get my robe on, try to call 911, call my neighbor and then collapse in a chair. God gives you strength at the right times.

Looking out the window was frightening but invigorating. I recognized many faces, but as I mentioned above there was a man who had on a red shirt and that was the reason the police wanted me to look out the window. I told the police I wasn't sure but in my heart he didn't seem to fit the physical description, as this guy had hair and the attacker didn't seem to have any or very little. Maybe he slipped on a toupee, so the police would have to question him. Turned out it was not the person as he apparently had an alibi where he was at the time of the rape. The police asked about Dave's whereabouts thinking something had happened between us. I know they had to ask about all possibilities but Dave's and my relationship is rock solid. I knew at that moment I needed Dave home as soon as possible. I asked the police if I could call his secretary and get a message to him that he needed to come home. I had to go to the hospital but wanted to make the phone call.

One of the officers made the call and I talked with Anita telling her to find Dave and request he return home. She asked me what was wrong, but not wanting to alarm her or Dave of the situation, I just said I wasn't feeling well and please have him call home. I felt bad about not saying more but can you imagine flying (driving) knowing your loved one had been raped and you weren't there? I just couldn't put Dave through that although I learned later that when he called home one of the officer's did tell him some of the facts.

Now is a good time to mention how I was treated by the police. With RESPECT! How wonderful. There was never an accusation or a demeaning word. They had nothing but encouraging words. I know some survivors have had different experiences and that is a shame. When I have talked with police groups or at the police academy, I have always emphasized the facts on how to treat the survivor. It takes courage just to get this far. The police must and should ask many questions and yes, personal. Reporting a rape is tough but it must be done. It's the only way the rapist can be caught.

Chapter Four

Once the ambulance arrived and the police had most questions asked and answered, place dusted for hand and shoe prints, I was asked if I was ready to go to the hospital for rape kit tests, etc. I was very ready to leave the house. The crowd outside was still there and the thought of anyone seeing me at this time was more than I wanted to bear. Fortunately, the driver was aware of my situation and asked if I would like to be covered (including my face). Definitely, but didn't want anyone to think I was dead. Apparently they spoke to the crowd to let them know I was OK. Many thoughts went through my head while riding in the back. Certainly was not the way I had imagined my day's events. The only good thing I could grasp was I was alive and how my life would be changed forever.....

Arriving at the hospital, things were ready. I was immediately taken to a private room in the ER and the process began. People in and out, taking blood pressure, my clothes (which were bagged in front of my eyes), temp, get a gown on and so on. The doctor was there in no time, I think even before the admitting clerk was there to take my personal information. The doctor was very concerned and professional throughout the whole examination. Questions were asked again about the rape, did I take a shower afterwards (no), in what areas did he hit me, did he ejaculate inside me and so many other questions that I really can't remember. They brought in a rape kit, which does include an injection for the prevention of HIV. Now that had never crossed my mind, but thank goodness they have the examination planned out in an orderly fashion. There was swelling, but no other harmful indications present. They swabbed the genital area for evidence, plucked hairs (now that hurts) from the pubic area and then I realized he had ejaculated on my stomach, so I asked them to take a swab in that area. Even though he had washed (reason for running water at the kitchen sink) the stomach, you never know if he might have missed a spot (Oh please let there be something).

While the doctor was finishing his exam, a social worker from the staff came in to talk about the rape. My neighbor had driven to the hospital behind the ambulance and I think she answered some questions. She was the only person there for me at the time. Lots of questions, but mostly how was I doing emotionally? I didn't have an answer, how was I doing? Nothing was sinking in, yet everything was as I couldn't focus. I know she was starting to irritate me. I wasn't dead, but I didn't feel very alive. My mind kept racing through the rape trying to think how I could have stopped such an act of hate. I know I did nothing wrong and never anything to promote such a disgusting act. I had to remember that rape is not about sex but power, but it sure didn't feel that way. I had been forced to do something that makes me sick to my stomach to this day. I knew I could never be the same but how was I going to explain that feeling. The social worker was patient (that's her job, of course) and explained their services. I was just not in a listening mood and finally had her moved out of the room. I must say, as was my experience with the police, everyone was very respectful and kind, never pointing a finger or making any comments that it must have been my fault; in the wrong place, wrong time, asking for it, and all the other hideous statements made about a rape victim.

The social worker told me the report would be sent to the police but I would be notified personally about the HIV report. If I had any other questions, feel free to call. I was now released. I had a message to be at the police station at 8:00 the next morning to meet with an officer.

Chapter Five

I had left phone numbers with the police before leaving the hospital so they could stay in contact with Dave through his office. He did call home and was informed of the situation. Toni took me to her house where I waited for Dave. I remember looking out her window at my once beautiful, beautiful house now hating the sight of it.

How Dave flew and then drove home all those hours knowing what had happened must have been horrible. Toni saw him park in the garage and then starting to walk towards her house when she ran out to talk with him before he came in. I had already started to cry, not stopping for a very long time. He looked like he had lost his very best friend. We didn't talk, just cried. Words would not come out and they were not needed.

After some time, we finally walked back to the house after thanking Toni for all she did and went through with me that day. I had a very hard time going through the front door. The police had done a great job of cleaning up their fingerprint dust, etc. I walked around for a while and then we sat on the sofa and I finally started to talk. We turned on the TV and the rape was reported on the 10 o'clock news on most Chicago stations. Then the phone calls started. Even though my name was not given, most of my friends figured out who it was as there were pictures of our neighborhood. I think the gal who had dropped me off after lunch felt guilty for leaving me. Who would have ever thought such a thing would happen to your friend in a neighborhood such as ours. I never spoke on the phone as Dave took all the calls. What a champ. Even his boss from Minneapolis called as he had heard from Dave's office in Chicago.

About midnight I took another bath. Don't know how many times I took one, but it was several. Guess I was trying to wash it all away. I kept scrubbing and scrubbing, thinking I could wash all the memories away. Dave stayed in the bathroom with me. Finally exhaustion put us to bed. Sleep? No way. I kept my eyes on the bedroom door, something I do to this day until I fall to sleep. I finally got up about four, took another bath, packed my clothes (lots of them) as I wanted to leave for Brentwood, TN after we had our meeting with the police. Dave got up and took Heine to the kennel. It was so hard to stay in the house alone, but necessary. That was the last time I ever slept in that house

Our meeting with the police was full of questions. The sergeant did make a statement that sort of threw me off. I have always and still do take great pride in my appearance and conduct. He commented that I looked very good for someone who had been through such an ordeal. I was still me and when I'm in public I try to look together with a sense of style. Should I have come in with sweats or my bathrobe on? No way. Remember you are still you and in no way should you let this rapist beat you down more than he already has done. Again we were treated well and Dave asked a lot of questions trying to understand what had been done and how we should move forward.

We left the station with positive thoughts. The hospital had identified some semen on my stomach and was turning it over to the FBI for DNA. It was very small and the police were hoping it would be enough to identify. We were so hopeful. Questions had been asked about my whereabouts that day. The gym for a workout (I went there three times a week) and maybe someone there had their eyes on me. We had stopped for lunch at a local Greek restaurant. We went there on several occasions and maybe someone there was watching me. Where did I shop, buy groceries, play golf and so on. They were going to look into everything. It had been reported that the younger neighborhood guy was being watched and questioned. He had done some landscaping work for us a few days prior to the rape and he was a possibility. He did fit the description somewhat as he was in his mid-twenties, tall and no hair. Plus he was a little odd acting at times. He had a questionable alibi but it didn't feel right to me because his dad said he smoked and that is something I did not smell. Turns out nothing ever became of this guy after weeks of questioning.

Chapter Six

We left the police station around 9:00 feeling they would do everything possible to find the rapist. We drove back to Brentwood, TN as planned. We had lived in Brentwood from 1985-1990. Dave had been transferred to the Chicago area to take over one of many Cargill steel facilities. I had really missed living in TN where our two daughters, Laura and Amy went to high school, graduated and attended Southern colleges. I had a great job in the travel industry and decided to give it up for a while due to our move to Chicago. Laura was married and Amy had graduated from Western Kentucky the previous year and was now newly engaged. We were coming back for an engagement congratulations gathering, seeing the ring for the first time. Coming back was like coming home again and very comfortable plus I needed to be with my whole family. We didn't mention what had happened the previous day as I didn't want to take the glory of Amy and Steve's special time. I'd deal with that later.

Before we left the police station that morning, they gave us several copies of the morning paper that had (as a headline) the story about the rape. I would approach that matter with the girls when it seemed fit.

We checked into our Brentwood hotel where Laura, Al and Amy were waiting at the bar. It was a glorious evening as we celebrated the engagement. Later, we would all go up to our suite to chat, knowing I would have to tell them about the rape. I could feel myself slipping into depression or maybe it was still shock. My opening would be to give them each a copy of the paper to read, not saying it was me. Seemed like hours while they all read the paper. My name was never mentioned, they were at first confused. Then, (I think it was Laura) said mom, was this you? Well you can imagine what transpired from there. Our daughters have always been very precious to us and as a close family, shared most everything. I never want to relive those hours again. Heartbreaking is the only way I can describe how the news affected all of them. It makes me cry just to write this, even now after all these years.

The girls decided to spend the night at the hotel. We had two queen beds, so the girls slept in one and Al went home to Nashville with our little granddaughter, Jess.

I think this night was the turning point for me that I needed more than family love. I woke up during the night screaming. I couldn't stop crying, knowing this person was coming back for me. I just could not deal with anything and desperately needed help. I will never forget Dave's statement as he sat up in bed. He said, "I don't know how to take care of her." No more sleep that night.

The next morning we decided I needed immediate help, probably a therapist. It was Labor Day weekend and how would we find anybody. Dave and the girls got the phone book and started looking for a number to call. They found a place called The Rape and Sexual Abuse Center listed. Luck would have it, when the call was made, a therapist (not a receptionist) Char answered the call. To this day, she is my angel, my savior and any other wonderful name I can think of and she truly saved my life. She chatted with Dave for quite some time and he made an appointment for me to see her following Tuesday. She was willing to stay late and come in that day, but I knew I could make it to Tuesday. Dave had already called my sister who lived in Washington State and would be there in a couple of days. We had decided not to mention this to my parents. This would probably put them under and I couldn't deal with explaining anything to someone who may feel worse than I did at this time.

Chapter Seven

My sister, Sharon arrived on Sunday and after a tearful reunion we went back to the hotel. The only thing I really remember was all the chatter in our hotel room and I finally had to escape. I asked Dave to take a walk with me as I needed his strength and stability. We walked a long time. It calmed me.

Tuesday arrived and Dave drove me to the Rape and Sexual Abuse Center. It was a big, old stately house in somewhat of a questionable area of Nashville. I walked in, gave my name and sat in the waiting area. I'll never forget the little boy who was playing with toys and thinking to myself why in the world would a small child be here. I assumed he was waiting for his mom who was in therapy. They called his name and he went into a therapy room. I was shocked but we all have to remember (and this I had to learn), rape can happen to anyone. I bring this topic into my speeches all the time. Rape does not discriminate...age, race, social standing, religion and any other title you want to put on a person. Children are especially vulnerable and that is so very sad.

I was called into a room that looked more like a nice sitting area with books lined up on the wall, comfy chairs, curtains on the windows and a feeling of being safe. A beautiful lady named Dr. Char Creson greeted me and asked me to have a seat in the comfy chair. The first thing

I noticed was a big box of Kleenex on the end table next to the chair.

The next hour went by so quickly, I hardly remember anything. Char never once asked me to talk about the rape. She concentrated on my emotions, feelings about myself and basically just let me cry (hence, the big box of Kleenex). She later commented that I looked like a little whipped puppy but knew I was a very strong person deep inside. This day was so very important to me and I cannot imagine going through the trauma I had experienced a few days prior and not seeking help. Please, please, please for all of you who have had the same experience, you need professional help. This is one time, no matter how long it has been, you need help.

Chapter Eight

In the state of Tennessee, you are allowed twelve weeks of therapy without monetary obligation. The Rape and Sexual Abuse Center is a nonprofit agency with some state support. Most of their support comes from private donations, community and corporate donations. Believe me they deserve every penny. Everything about the Center is very professional with lots of love and concern. I faithfully went every week, usually at times wanting to be there more than an hour. I felt safe and this is where the healing begins.

The next six weeks I lived at the hotel. I spent many days visiting the Nashville Parthenon talking to Athena, the Greek goddess of wisdom. Dave had to go back to work in Chicago, so Amy moved in with me. She worked at Gaylord Entertainment Center in the marketing department, so suffered through a long drive from Brentwood every day. Not only did she sacrifice her independence, but at 23 years old, she had to become the adult. I was in no shape to be living alone nor was I emotionally stable. Plus she was trying to be excited about her upcoming wedding the following fall. Laura always stopped by after work to check on me. It was a pleasure to see her and my little Jess, so happy and innocent. We would eventually learn Laura was pregnant with David, a blessing at this time. (This is the part of the book that Laura and Amy need to express in words and emotions.) Also many of my close friends came over, sometimes going out to lunch, playing golf or just talking. Yes, I told everyone. I never once felt embarrassed to talk about my rape, knowing it was not my fault. No one ever asks to be raped no matter the situation. This is a subject that is faithfully taught to you during therapy. How anyone can live with this for years privately is beyond comprehension.

Dave flew back to Nashville every Friday and would go back on Monday mornings. What a wonderful company he worked for as they gave us all the support needed. I knew I could never go back to the house we lived in, something we would eventually have to work out.

One of the first weekends in Brentwood, we were invited to a very close couple friend's house. We had not said anything to them when we received the invitation. I had come back to Brentwood frequently to see the girls, granddaughter and our friends. Plus I had kept in touch with my travel friends and still planned and implemented some private group trips, therefore, not unusual that I was in town. We sat on the patio chatting aimlessly having a glass of wine. All of a sudden the constant chatter got to me and I dropped the glass on wine on the cement, which shattered and startled all of us. Lots of noise seemed to get to me very quickly as I always feared that person would sneak up behind me and I wouldn't be ready to defend myself. Of course, everything spilled out of my mouth with help from Dave. They were genuinely shocked but concerned. Another reason to tell is that people can and will embrace the worst news and stay by your side.

David phoned another one of our couple friends and they were at our door in no time. We have had and still have wonderful friends and let me tell you when I say they will not judge you. Remember you cannot do any type of recovery by yourself which I constantly state throughout this book. It is important if you are one who is living with your private secret.

Chapter Nine

After a few weeks in therapy, Char asked me if I would speak to a group of doctors, nurses, EMT's, and hospital workers, telling them my story and stating how important their treatment can make as an impression on the survivor's recovery. Wow, that sounded scary to me as I didn't know if I could tell my story without breaking down a hundred times and still get a very important point across. Well, let me tell you, not only did I get through the speech (yes, lots of tears) but I seemed to gain strength with their many questions and concerns. Then the Executive Director of the Center, Tim Tohill asked me to speak to the Board. Now this one really threw me off because I was one of the reasons they did fund raising for the Center and what if I didn't come off in the right tone. Again, during my talk I fell apart and truly was thinking I'll never get well if I keep this up. Towards the end of my speech I started noticing several members wiping tears from their face including some guys. This is probably the moment I realized I had a real calling for getting a very important subject out beyond the therapy walls. I hugged Tim after the speech and thanked him for putting me on center stage with my story. This began my quest to help as many survivors as possible.

I had been asking God why this had happened to me. I grew up with great parents, nice Christian home, many friends, college educated and my own wonderful husband and daughters. I was in a career that I really liked. My life was comfortable and happy (I was 47 at the time of the rape). Well, after the speech I found the answer. Maybe God had chosen me to be the spokesperson for rape survivors as I certainly could speak from experience. It happened to me so I could go out and help others that were dealing with rape and personal shame. Most survivors feel somehow to blame or they think others will feel that way. I would have rather had someone else have this role, but I got the job. I am a true believer in God and my faith remains very strong. I have had some very weak moments as not only does this affect the survivor, but the whole family. Dave, Laura and Amy will give their honest thoughts in another chapter. I doubt the rapist realizes how much damage he does as he goes about his daily living, maybe even thoughts of another rape. He not only raped me, he raped my family.

    As the time moved on, the local Brentwood police stayed on any news from the Dyer police. They were so good about calling and just checking in with me. Reports from the north looked grim as there was no news, although the following month there was another rape reported of a nurse with some of the same chain of events. We never received a report from the FBI regarding the small amount of semen they had found on my stomach. Dave thinks they lost it in the hospital or on its way to the lab. I will tell you now after 17 years, the rapist has never been caught. Does this bother me? Yes, in some ways it still does but I decided I had to go on and start living my life again. No way was that guy going to take my freedom and resilience away from me. I just had to learn to cope in different ways. I am constantly on my guard to this day. Sometime people surprise me on their habits, especially leaving their garage door open when working around the outside perimeter of their house. Anyone can slip in so quickly.

Chapter Ten

Public speaking and TV spots regarding rape became my strength as the weeks and months passed by. I had gone back to work in the travel industry, something that had been a part of me since the late 70's. I took a non-management position as I didn't feel ready for any responsibility. I had travelled the world with incentive groups and wanted to prove to myself I could go on with this passion, but not yet. Amy and I had moved from the hotel into a two bedroom apartment while Dave put our home for sale up north, traveling back and forth every weekend. This is where I need to express my gratitude to our son-in-law, Al, who checked in with me every day and on weekends along with Laura. I still wasn't ready to have Amy leave me. Sometimes I look back at this decision and think how selfish I was to make her my keeper. She needed to move on, but I just couldn't let her go. I know Laura and Dave were trying to do as much as possible but my insecurities about being alone still haunted me. Dave's company was working towards the possibility of transferring him back to the Nashville location. He really was the one that decided to give up so much as far as his career. He had been general manager of two locations for many years, but when we were transferred to the Chicago, the Nashville spot had to be filled. There had to be many decisions for Dave, while he remained very supportive of me. All I knew was I could not go back to Chicago to live and yet I missed him so much As I said before, the rapist does not realize how his disgusting actions turn a whole family upside down.

In November I received a call from my Aunt LaVonne (Mom's sister) telling me that Mom's Hepatitis C had taken a turn for the worse and I needed to come home. She said she was very curious why I hadn't been home for a while as Mom's health had not been good the last couple of months. I had still been calling home weekly, but kept the conversation pointed towards their activities. My mom found out about twenty years earlier that she had the disease which was treatable but not curable. We never really knew how she got Hepatitis C.

I told my aunt on the phone the whole story, which of course shocked her. Not wanting to tell Mom and Dad (in their seventies), I asked her to keep my story to herself as she did very faithfully. I did go back to northern Iowa where my parents lived and received the bad news from Mom's doctor that she only had at the most six months to live. How was I going to deal with all of this sadness that was settling into our lives? Maybe this would distract me from the rape by putting all my strength into my parent's life. I spent the next four months flying back and forth from Brentwood.

Dave was finally offered a wonderful position with his company back in Nashville and on February 3rd, we moved into our present home in Brentwood. A lovely home, where I could feel safe and still do every day. Unfortunately, while the furniture was being unloaded, Amy had gotten a call at work that I needed, once again, to come home. Thanks to my wonderful daughters and friends, the house got organized in my absence. I stayed at the hospital daily with my mom until the 12th of February when my sister and brother-in-law arrived from Washington. Getting back to Brentwood was comforting until the 15th, when Heine suddenly passed away. Sadly, Mom passed away on the 25th. My sweet Heine, now Mom. I stayed in Iowa for another two weeks along with my sister helping Dad get through some very difficult times. Since the end of August, nothing was making any sense. Why was I raped and why did my mom die while she was still in the prime of her life? I knew at this point I had to get back into helping every rape victim, helping the Center get the word out to all who would listen. I was now on the war path to vindicate every survivor by stressing that abuse had to be reported.

Chapter Eleven

The following ten years changed for me in many ways. I got back into the travel industry planning personal as well as group travel. I started to escort group again in many parts of the USA plus the Caribbean and internationally. One area that was really hard for me was the Grand Bazaar in Istanbul, Turkey. People were very friendly but as you walked through the Bazaar, many Turkish men who wore red shirts would come out of their stalls trying to sell you something. I finally had to leave as it was so crowded, noisy and those red shirts were way beyond intolerable at this point of my life. Actually, it is still hard for me to look at a man in a red shirt. I was gone on this trip for 18 days and felt maybe I had pushed a little too hard and fast regarding my recovery. In time I got better and better, I realized this was going to be a part of my life if I wanted to stay in the industry and do what I did best. I did retire in 2004 from travel to work more with the Center and pursue other interest.

During the years I tried at every turn to speak to groups when requested. The United Way of Williamson County has an incredible staff and their calls to me were always answered in the positive. The Center asked me on different occasions to speak to groups, such as judges, lawyers, police, etc. Plus I spoke to corporations, privately held groups, retail, etc. I also answered calls from the media (TV, newspapers, radio) when a rape occurred in the area or legislative changes brought attention to victims and survivors. This was always through the Center first and then passed on to me for permission.

I will always have a great big place in my heart for the Sexual Abuse Center and their wonderful staff. The years have been good, blessing my life with Dave and now we have five wonderful grandchildren, Jessica, David, Zach, Noah and Joseph.

I have also tried to find "why" this horrible experience happened to me. I know I said earlier that maybe I had answered that question, but after going through my story I now think it was not to find the "why" but the "because". Because I was raped, I know I was/am an instrument in God's plan for me. Helping others accept and go on with their lives is my mission. If this book can help one individual, I have truly accomplished the purpose of this book. If it helps many, even better. Maybe the trickle-down theory will apply. I help one person, they help another and so on. Getting someone to talk about this (out of the box so to speak) can change their life for the positive. The rape should not shape what you are but who you want to be...a very strong person that is not ashamed and to remember the worst thing is never the last thing. In the words of Adam Hamilton, "Sometimes when we are the weakest, we are the strongest."

The Final Chapter

Why call this book "Purple Mums"? After all that had happened, many speeches on survival and encouragement, I was still missing something. I don't buy the idea of closure. What does that mean anyway? There are many things in your life that you can live with, but not forget, therefore no closure. Well, maybe a chapter but not the whole book.

I still, after 17 years, watch where I sit in a restaurant. I am very aware of my surroundings, noting who is around me. I remember when I was at work at a large travel agency we had a meeting regarding security. The head of human resources (who was a good friend) was talking about being mindful of your surroundings. During the course of her speech, a guy walked into the room, handed her a pink slip of paper and walked out. He was there maybe thirty seconds. She finished her talk and then handed everyone a blank piece of paper. She asked that everyone list as many features we could remember about the guy who came in earlier. Clothing, looks, any conversation he had with the leader, etc. Most people listed 10 or less items. I had over 20 items and won by a large margin. Unbelievable how aware I am since the rape. This is a good thing.

Now, why did I name the book "Purple Mums". On my 10th anniversary of the rape I wanted to do something special to celebrate this milestone. I thought about going on a cruise with friends and family. I had also thought about having a big party at our house to celebrate. Next thought was to get away with Dave. Nothing sounded good to me. In ten years I had refused to buy any kind of purple flowers, especially mums. That is what I was planting the day of the rape.

As time was getting closer to the 31st of August, I was getting agitated with myself on how I would handle the 10th year. Then it hit me.

On the 31st, I got up and went to the nursery. There I bought two large purple mum plants. Brought them home, planted them and at 2:00, I sat outside on my glider and remembered how much I had accomplished in 10 years. I had come full circle from that day, saying I would never plant another purple mum. I was so proud of myself, proud of my quest to help as many victims and survivors as possible and try to inspire people in the general public to be aware of their surroundings. Very proud of my family and proud in my faith in God who gave me all the strength and ability to take something so tragic and turn it into a positive.

DAVE

"…all I could think of was Sandy…"

Some of these memories are probably not completely accurate as this is being written 15 years later. I am writing this without confirming any of the details with Sandy. It is not uncommon that her memories today are much more accurate than mine.

My experience began mid- afternoon in northeast Iowa. I was riding with our sales representative heading to a customer in Mason City. Cell phone service was spotty in many rural parts of the country, including this area. A call came through from Anita, our administrative assistant. It was barely audible and all that came through was "emergency" and that we needed to talk. I tried to tell her we would call back from the first pay phone we could find. At that time, pay phones were common at all gas stations. I assumed that there had been some kind of accident in the plant. While still a major concern, it didn't occur to me that it was about Sandy.

It was probably between a half and 1 hour before we finally got to a phone and back in contact with the office. It was then that Anita explained that Sandy had called and been attacked, that the police were involved and that Sandy was alive. Flights to Chicago had been checked and the only firm reservation was later that evening. However, there was a stand-by possibility departing non-stop from Waterloo (next to where I grew up) that was leaving within a couple of hours that they had booked for me.

I believe I was able to then talk to Sandy at our home. She sounded dazed. She said the police and emergency people were there and that she had been tied up, threatened with a knife to her throat and raped – but she was alive. They were about to take her to the hospital.

I made it on the stand-by flight from Waterloo to Chicago O'Hare. Connie Hauswirth, our Administrative Manager, picked me up as my car was at Midway airport. She got me to the car and I drove home. Sandy had been released and was at a neighbor's house. I went to the neighbors and then Sandy and I went home. It was around 9-10. One vivid memory was seeing our normally calm neighborhood with a news helicopter flying over our house. Details of the evening are not as clear today. Sandy spent most of the evening describing what had happened and I tried to provide comfort and reassurance. Another clear memory was that we were sitting in the family room and the TV was on quietly. All of a sudden the 10 pm news came on and here was Sandy's story as the headline news in Chicago. I thought, "Things are really bad when you are the evening news lead story in Chicago."

Around 11pm, the phone rang and it was my boss, Ty Thayer, who lived in Minneapolis checking to see how we were. We talked for a couple of minutes and then he handed the phone to his wife, Kit. I sensed that it was too emotional for him to continue. We filled her in on what had happened. She said that Ty would call the next day.

We spent the following day talking with the police. They were searching for any connection that we might be able to think of that could lead them to the perpetrator. I also talked with the office where everyone assured me that they could handle things. Ty also called. I told him that we were planning to head back to Tennessee as soon as the police were done with us. He said that Cargill would be fully behind us and not to worry about time away from the office as he knew I was always in touch.

We were able to return to Nashville the next day. Our son-in-law, Aleks, was a manager at a local hotel and got us a room at a greatly reduced rate. That became our home away from home for the next few weeks. Our youngest daughter, Amy, was working at Gaylord Entertainment and living with friends in an apartment east of Nashville. Her lease expired shortly after we returned to Nashville and she and Sandy ended up in an apartment near the airport.

After a couple of weeks, I returned to Indiana and put the house on the market. We decided that I would continue to live there until it sold. At that point, I became a weekend commuter. Thank goodness for Southwest Airlines. They had several non-stop flights each way daily between Nashville and Midway Airport. It quickly became a routine to depart Midway every Friday afternoon and depart Nashville every Monday morning. While I would have done it at any price, Southwest would have fairly regular sales @ $49 per flight (I believe that was round trip). I would buy 10 flights at a time. When last minute changes occurred, I could use a free frequent flyer ticket so the overall commute cost was reasonable.

Over the next few weeks in Indiana, I had a number of meetings with the local police and a meeting or two with county or state officials and 1 or 2 meetings with the FBI. There was no specific suspect. There were several men in the area that had sexual assault histories, but over time most of them were eliminated. The FBI got involved because a convicted serial rapist had escaped from an Ohio prison a couple of days before Sandy was attacked and his trail appeared to go our direction. As the investigation continued, the police found footsteps and other indications that the attacker appeared to have been watching Sandy from behind a hill of dirt located on the empty wooded lot next to our house. During one meeting the officials asked me if I felt the union at our plant could have been a factor in any way. I realize they had to pursue all angles, but I told them then and still believe today that our plant union folks were as caring, supporting and empathetic with what we were going through as anyone we had contact with.

The prime suspect, in our minds, was the adult son who lived with his parents several houses down the street from us. He fit Sandy's description of a normal height, slightly built younger man. We never had much contact with him or the family. I don't remember any specifics to support that memory. I know the police questioned him and couldn't get anything to take action. He walked and still rode a bike in the neighborhood even though he could drive. After Sandy had returned to Nashville, he actually rode by when I was mowing the lawn a couple of times and tried to start a conversation. I would have nothing to do with him. The local police constantly cruised by our house and as a result, I had regular discussions with them. They all seemed to take personally what had happened to Sandy and I felt they would do anything possible to help me. A few weeks later the neighbor's son was cleared of any charges.

The fall months went by pretty quickly in kind of a blur. Two clear memories of that time were:

While I was returning to Tennessee on Friday, I was already dreading the thought of Monday when I had to leave Sandy, our family and Tennessee and return to Indiana. On the way to the airport Monday mornings, I was already beginning to long for Fridays when I could return. There were five of us that commuted to Chicago on the 1st Southwest Airlines flight every Monday for most of the time I made the trip. Every Monday we would look at each other and say that there has got to be a better way to live one's life.

The other memory from that time is that it seemed while at work all I could think of was Sandy all day and what we were going through. When I got home at night I could not sleep and would worry about what was happening at work. During the 9 months of evenings in Indiana, I believe I read all the James Michener books at least once and a couple of them a second time. While I could sleep when I was back in Tennessee on the weekends, the average night's sleep during the week was probably a couple of hours.

There was some buyer interest in our house during the fall but activity dropped off in November and December. I was able to use the evenings to go through all the boxes of stuff we had accumulated over the years. It was interesting to find 1 box that had 3 moving stickers on it and obviously had not been opened since the 1st sticker. The contents were from a kitchen "junk" drawer and an adjoining cupboard. I remember that there was at least 1 item that we had wondered where it had disappeared. This was a good time to clean out a lot of items which went to Goodwill and the garbage.

During Christmas week, we received an offer on the house. It turns out it was from a local family who had toured the house shortly after it was listed and decided as a strategy to wait until Christmas week to make an offer. They knew the builder and had looked at the house before we bought it (from the builder who was living in it) and had always wanted it. After some negotiations, we got the offer up to an acceptable price and sold the house. The closing was out a few weeks to give them time to sell their home and allow us time to find a home in Tennessee.

We found our current home in Tennessee in January. It was vacant as it had been sold a month earlier to a couple from Indianapolis who wanted to move closer to their kids. One of them had health issues that worsened after they had purchased the house. They decided to stay in Indianapolis near their doctor(s) and we were able to purchase the house with immediate availability. We had toured several houses and while some were possibilities, when we walked into our current home for the first time, Sandy said "this is it."

Closings on both houses occurred roughly February 1, 1995. The moving began. An apartment was rented in Schererville IN, a few miles from our old house for my Indiana residence. I rented a U-Haul in Indiana and with some help from folks at work, moved the items I needed from our old house to the Indiana apartment. We then loaded the U-Haul with items that movers wouldn't carry and I drove to Tennessee. Once the U-Haul was unloaded at our new Tennessee home with the items from Indiana, we then loaded it with all the items from the Tennessee apartment and moved them to the new home. Our neighbors told us a few years later that they actually thought that I worked for U-Haul. For the normal stuff, we were able to use the Cargill contract movers even though this was a personal move. I don't remember who the Cargill moving coordinator was, but she explained what we were going through to the movers and she and the moving company were fabulous in helping us through this period. We may have even received a better rate than the typical corporate rate.

Finally, by the end of a couple of weeks of moving, we were in our house. I have fond memories of the many people both in Tennessee and Indiana who helped us through this trying time.

As if there had not been enough strain, we received a call during the week of moving in, that Sandy's mother, who had been ill for some time, had taken a turn for the worse in Iowa. At nearly the same moment, our 14 year old miniature dachshund died. Sandy, Laura, Amy and Laura's husband, Aleks, buried Heine in the back yard one evening that first week during a heavy rain storm. Sandy's mom died at the end of February.

It felt normal again when I was in Tennessee on weekends in our own home with Sandy and Amy. The next few weeks/months were kind of a blur. We greatly enjoyed the weekends and met and began to spend time with great new neighbors. I continued to commute each week to the plant in northwest Indiana. I traveled quite a bit out of our Indiana plant as the apartment was depressing. I had moved fast to find a clean, reasonable sized, cheap apartment. While it fit all those conditions, I never realized how depressing old gold shag carpet and dark wood paneling in a lower level apartment complex could be. Evenings dinners in the apartment were typically a "healthy" microwave dinner, low fat cookies and scotch. The great weekends offset the difficult weeks.

Several months passed with this situation. Jim Thompson replaced Ty Thayer as our division President. After some meetings, during a sit down, Jim observed that the current situation was not working out and he had a proposal. Would I give up my position as manager of the East Chicago plant? As a general manager, I had always been closely involved with the commercial side of our business and knew many of the key customers for both the Nashville and East Chicago operations. I would become the sales manager for both facilities. I could spend every other week in Tennessee and when I was in Indiana, I could stay in a hotel. The company would now cover all travel expenses. The Vice President Title and rewards would go but I would keep the same salary and cover both facilities. The job required a lot of travel but I was used to that. It also saved the company money as they would not have to have two sales managers. It was an easy decision and I believe I agreed on the spot. So in August 1995, I became the General Sales Manager for locations, living in Tennessee and spending every other week in Indiana. Much of the time for both plants was spent traveling with sales representatives calling on customers.

A couple of months later, Jim surprised me when he asked that I submit all the relocation expenses we had paid for in the move back to Tennessee and they were completely reimbursed by Cargill. Our situation was beginning to look a lot better.

I continued to work for the East Chicago facility every other week for approximately nine months with every other week at the plant or traveling to visit their customers. While this was a great improvement in time at home for a while, in time the same dread of heading back to East Chicago started to return. Not only that, it was hard on both locations to have a sales manager for a week and then have him gone for a week. By the next spring, I had decided that I needed to get back to Tennessee full time but was uncertain how it might be received. Cargill management had supported us through a difficult personal time and I felt guilty about asking for another change. In fact, I was uncertain enough about the reaction that I had discussions with some other companies (customers, not competitors) about availability of jobs if my only option was to take another job. Fortunately, at least one company made a legitimate enough offer that I felt comfortable enough to ask Cargill for consideration. As it turned out, everyone thought it made sense. I took a pay cut to be in line with compensation levels for a single location sales manager. But Sandy was working again (she quit when we moved to Indiana) and was offsetting a good share of the cut. I was now back to Tennessee full time and life began to feel a bit more normal from a work perspective.

During all the activities, no progress was made in identifying or capturing the fugitive that raped Sandy.

While my memories of work dates is somewhat accurate, other dates tended to get lost with all the running around that was occurring. I don't remember when I first got in contact with the Nashville Rape and Sexual Abuse Center. I believe it was shortly after getting back to Nashville. We were directed to Char Creson to counsel Sandy. Char was a special (to us) counselor that had worked with Sandy and spent some time with me. While Sandy had worked with Char for some time, I believe it was several weeks later before I actually met with her. I had been so busy trying to hold things together functionally that I had shoved the experience into a mental corner and had not really dealt with it. While my experience and emotions didn't hold a candle to what Sandy had gone through, Char helped me realize that talking about my feelings would not only help me, but would help me be a better support for Sandy. One thing that did change for me was my empathy for others. I had trained myself over the years at work to stay focused on the objectives and goals for me and the organization. As a result, I did not have much sympathy for others that had personal challenges at work. I couldn't understand how family issues would cause someone to have to miss or be late for work. If someone had reoccurring issues, then it was up to us to find someone who could do the job without family issues. Two things dramatically changed my outlook. One was realizing that neither Sandy nor I had done anything to deserve what she had to endure when she was attacked. It was an eye opener as I always felt that folks with personal or family problems just hadn't prepared properly to handle them. It became painfully obvious that conditions can change regardless of your personal actions and that you do not have control of everything that happens to you. The other thing that had a huge impact on me was learning how many other people handled personal tragedy with quiet strength and determination. As word spread about our experience, I was amazed how many coworkers, customers and suppliers offered their own stories as an example of how one can handle personal challenges. I got to the point where I felt almost everyone I came in contact with had some type of life altering experience that would have broken down any average person. All these people had or were handling their issues with unbelievable strength.

As a result of the meetings with Char, we were introduced to a number of folks from the Rape and Sexual Abuse Center. Early on we met Tim Tohill, RSAC's director. After a couple of meetings, Tim explained that the Center was considering a move from the small house that they were operating from and would I consider becoming involved with a small group that was looking for options. Before long, I was actively involved with a small group involved in the building and meeting a number of others connected to the Center. In a fairly short time, a new building was identified and purchased and a major fund raising effort was begun. Somewhere during this period, I was asked if I would consider becoming a board member, which I accepted.

Several things occurred during the fundraising that was amazing. Both of our daughters, Laura and Amy always were close to what was happening with us (mostly their mom). We were blessed to have Laura living within 5 minutes of us. While we were blessed to have Amy with us when we first moved back to Nashville, she had since married Steve and moved to the Atlanta area. After moving, Amy had gone to work for Pamico, a large heating and air conditioning distributer in Atlanta. She blew us all away when she called one day to advise that Pamico would supply all new heating and air conditioning equipment and would work with a local HVAC company to have it all installed at no cost to RSAC. Secondly, Cargill had a program to support local nonprofit companies. The maximum a local Cargill business could donate to a nonprofit per year and receive a corporate match was $3,000 x 2 = $6000. Cargill stepped up and did that for 3 years in a row, the maximum number of years you could request for a matching donation. Leggett & Platt was a longtime customer with a couple of divisions in Nashville. We did a lot of business with one division. The other division made a contribution of $5,000. While the division we knew well denied any involvement, I always wondered if there was some connection. Additionally, a number of individuals we knew made personal donations. We had made annual contributions to the Center but never expected that others would join us to the extent that they did.

Sometimes one struggles to find the "silver lining" when you experience the type of event that Sandy did. However, there have been several "silver linings".

Seeing the real strength that can come when one faces unexpected personal tragedies

Sandy became involved as a speaker for United Way and RSAC about her experience and the help the RSAC can bring. As a result she has helped many people and heals a little bit more with every telling.

I became more sensitive and more sensitive to others which has made me a better person.

We have met many fine people as a result our association with RSAC – especially Char and Tim.

I realized that many of the people we interact with every day have their own personal challenges that they are meeting with quiet strength. I now appreciate that.

Most importantly, Sandy and I became closer as a result of all of this and no one can ever take that away.

Today we still support the Center financially with a donation every year and expect to continue to do so in the future. No amount of contributions can repay the help that they gave us.

LAURA

My Rock

ROCK—Any strong, solid person or thing, often acting as a support, refuge, defense, etc. (Webster's Dictionary).

That is my mom. My name is Laura and I am Sandy's oldest daughter. Mom called me tonight and asked me again, to submit my chapter for this book. The first time she asked me was several months ago or maybe it was a year ago, but it is now crunch time and she needs my chapter. Truth be told, I have sat down several times to write, but never finished. It is hard for me. I am famous for many excuses and why I cannot complete things that are asked of me. If it is something I want to do – it is done immediately, but when it comes to facing emotions I tend to brush it off. I am the first to admit that.

FAMILY – Our family has always been close. As long as I can remember, Thanksgiving and Christmas holidays and all summers would include my grandparents and extended relatives in Iowa and Minnesota. Our family often spent time in northern Minnesota – what great memories. Mom and dad would take Amy and me as kids, and as our families grew, we all still went. No matter where we lived, my parents always made family their top priority. That priority continues to this day. My youngest sister, Amy, and her husband, Steve, have three boys, and Alex and I have a daughter and son. Mom and dad always make it a point to spend quality time with each of them individually, doing whatever the kids want to do. In my opinion, it is family bonds that hold it all together. In addition to the grandkids, mom is our sounding board. We can call her at any time of the day for advice, to vent, or just want her shoulder to cry on.

MARRIAGE – Mom and dad have an incredible relationship. The love between the two of them is what we all strive for in a marriage. They were married young with two girls. Dad worked two jobs, continued his education, and mom took care of us –the way she always does. The odds were against them, but they made it work. In my opinion, mom and dad represent true love. I never realized how strong their bond was.

I could not write my chapter without background on our family and how close we are. I think it is very relevant as to how "the incident" affected us.

I had never heard my father cry – until the first night when they told us what happened. That rocked my world. Amy and I were sitting at the hotel bar, having a few beverages and waiting. Mom and dad show up with a bell cart full of clothes. Kisses were exchanged, and silence. We all went to the room, and that is where we were told of what happened. All I can remember of that night is hearing mom's screams in her sleep and dad crying trying to console her. I cannot describe to you what emotions that brought out to us kids. I have to say that was the worst night of my life.

Mom took up residence in a local hotel. The house was put on the market in Chicago; dad commuted back and forth and even took a demotion to come back to Nashville. Since Amy was single and working, she and mom rented an apartment. I have to say that I am so proud of my sister for being there for mom when I couldn't. I was married with a young daughter and pregnant with my son. I would visit as much as I could, but was not there with mom full time like Amy. Mom was in therapy, and Amy worked full time and came home each evening to take care of mom. I gained a lot of respect for Amy at that point. She is much stronger than I am.

That point refers to the first paragraph in my chapter. I am not good with facing tough situations head on. I believe that I created my "bubble" when mom was raped. Notice that this is the first time I used that word. I hate that word.

The Sexual Assault Center and those who work there are life lines to those who reach out for help. The care and support my mom and dad received from them was invaluable. I have attended several events there, and I always leave speechless. I think it is so important for victims to reach out for help. After months of therapy, mom decided to become a voice. She threw herself into the spotlight speaking whenever she could. I believe that is what helps her heal – helping others. Not being ashamed and what happened to her could happen to anyone.

To sum it up, my mom is my rock. She is stronger than any person that I have ever known. She is always there for me as well as my family, and I am so proud of her.

I love you mom.

AMY

My Hero

Do you have a hero? I did. It was my mom. She has been through an awful ordeal. But, she should be your inspiration, she is mine. You too can come out of this the way she has.

It was the first weekend in September. I was living in Nashville and my sister and her family lived there as well. My parents were living in a suburb of Chicago, my dad's company kept my parents on the move. Just out of college I was a 23 year old just trying to get by, but desperately in love. My love lived in Atlanta and we had gotten engaged the weekend of the 19th of August. That date is squarely in between both of our birthdays, so it was perfect. What a perfect birthday present. Mom was always good about coming to visit for our birthdays. She was supposed to come in on Friday night and it was Thursday, she called to say she was coming a day early and that my dad was coming too, unusual, but cool nonetheless. We would meet as we always do at the hotel where my brother-in-law works and where my mom would stay sometimes when she came in town. This hotel was special to us; it is where my sister fell in love with her husband, where they got married and where we would go sometimes in high school to have "gatherings". My sister and I were sitting at the bar waiting for them to come, having a humorous conversation, my parents walk in, excited to see them, we jump off the bar stools and give hugs and kisses. They are so excited about my engagement ring and we have casual conversation. Dad offers to get a six pack and take it up to the room so we can have a beer and chat. This is not unusual. We go up to the room and they say nothing but give us a copy of a newspaper article. The article states there was a woman home alone and an unidentified man had broken into the house while she was outside planting mums and watched her from room to room. Upon her entering the home, he attacked her and raped her. Not knowing if I was reading the right article, I remember thinking "That is horrible; I wonder why I am reading this". I went on reading, there was a miniature dachshund dog that tried to help her but was swept away by the intruder. The moment hit like a ton of bricks. The moment our lives would never again be the same. My mother had been raped. Hysteria ensued with questions and confusion as both my mother and father burst into tears. "My father is crying". I thought, I had only seen him cry once in my life. We sat there in disbelief. Relieved that she is okay, but confused!

My sister didn't take the news well, just cried. Laura and I decided we needed to be with our family that night. We stayed at the hotel. The middle of the night, my mom is screaming. My dad wakes up crying...what do you do? Sympathy, confusion. My parents are my rocks, my role models. What do you do when you have to be the strong one??? What did I do? I got them water and coffee and did not know what to do. Just talk to them. She is having nightmares. Dad feels guilty he was out of town when this happened. Laura lives in a bubble of happiness. She was out on the back porch wrapped up in a blanket rocking in the fetal position. The first few days were days of realization and feeling of not knowing where to go or what to do. I don't know how long we were there, but it seemed like an eternity. We would try to go on about our business and go back to work and come to the hotel at night. We contacted the Rape and Sexual Abuse Center of Nashville to see what we could do. Mom was immediately placed in therapy and met with a counselor. We would go out to dinner and talk, she wasn't the same person. Where was my career oriented person that didn't back down from a challenge, the person I emulated my life after? Who was this crumpled person in the corner chair? We would go out and we would all have a few drinks and when she got really bad, she would call her sister and have mini breakdowns. So much so that I worried that her sister would think this is the way she always was. So I called her and explained that when the visions and dreams got really bad, she called her sister and so she decided to come and help us take care of mom. We would get up in the morning and have breakfast and she and dad would take a little walk. Then what? Mom didn't want to go too many places, because she always had the fear that this person was lurking in the distance. The only way to make her feel safer was to walk behind her. Definitely no sneaking up on her!! Growing up, on the weekends, we went shopping, to fairs, all public places. Now that option was out. So there we sat in the hotel room, quietly going crazy! My fiancé would come up on the weekends sometimes and I would go down to Atlanta to visit him. My dad would fly back on the weekends to stay with mom. We stayed in the hotel for 6 weeks. I was finishing my last class in college at a remote place, working full time and taking care of my mom. Fortunately, the lease on my apartment was up and I could move in with my mom and help to take care of her.

 I came back from a weekend with my fiancé and my parents had rented an apartment for my mom and me to move into. They were very supportive of my privacy; they got us a two bedroom with two separate entrances. This would have been great. Except a new part of our daily living was to inspect the entire apartment, closets and all each time we walked in the apartment. This made twice as difficult with the two entrances. The schedule was getting a little more stable. Mom has always been a career woman and she was desperately trying to get back to "normal". She decided to get a job. Having a career as a travel agent was her passion. She was still having little breakdowns now and then and defiantly was having challenges getting through the day, but staying home and dwelling was not her thing. She went out and got a job she was over qualified for, but something she could handle at the time. So here we were, taking it one day at a time, dad visiting on the weekends.

We are trying to plan a wedding and my sister is pregnant. I was so thankful to have a few good things to look forward to, my mom in counseling. Things were very difficult for her, her confidence in the world was gone. One thing she insisted on was continuing to go to church. Every Sunday we went, we sobbed. What was going on? I am 23 years old and having panic attacks every day. What was I supposed to do? Who do I turn to? I literally didn't know how I was going to get through each day. I wasn't sleeping because I too was so afraid that this person was going to come and try to find her. I am taking care of my mother and my dad, working full time, trying to finish college and plan a wedding. How much more could be on my shoulders.

No matter what I was going through would never, ever amount to what my mother was going through, so why should I complain. Except that I was not functioning!!! I decided I need to start planning my wedding. I did some research and found some wedding boutiques and went one day after work. I walked into the boutique and looked around. I tried on a few dresses. I tried one on and loved it. Why was I so sad and anxiety ridden? I broke down that day in the wedding dress boutique. I was mad, sad, full of anxiety, tired and confused. I was standing in a wedding boutique trying on wedding dresses as this was supposed to make me happy. My mom should be here with me, I am not supposed to be here alone. Why couldn't my mom, my old mom, my confident mom, my rock be here with me? Why am I looking at wedding dresses by myself? IT IS NOT SUPPOSED TO BE LIKE THIS!!!!! I should not be taking care of my mom; she has always taken care of me. Why is she broken? Why does my dad turn to me for advice? Where is my sister? I had so many emotions and as I sit here writing this I cry for that 23 year old standing in that bridal boutique.

It wasn't fair that some son of a bitch took my mom away and they can't catch him. Why am I the strong one? It is all wrong. I think I sat in my car for 30 minutes having a total anxiety attack. I did not realize at the time what was going on. I needed counseling. I tell you all of this because everyone that goes through this is in desperate need of help, but...so is the support!!!!! The rape happened to my mom, but it happened to all of us.

The weeks and the months passed on. I would come home from work every day and sit at the table and talk to my mom, the anxiety attacks ensued almost daily. It was getting worse for both of us.

My fiancé and I decide we needed to get away with our friends to go skiing over New Years. We left and the weekend did help somewhat, just getting away. When we got back, my parents had bought a house in Brentwood, deciding mom was not going back to the Chicago area and they were somehow, someway going to get back to living where she felt safe. I think that was a huge help not having to go back to where it all happened. She was lucky. Mom and I moved into the house. The day for moving in was upon us, we thought a new start. My dad had started the process of changing his schedule and moving back to Brentwood as he stayed up at his apartment during the week in Chicago. The phone rings, it is my aunt and she tells me my grandmother (mom's mom) has been taken by ambulance to the hospital. She has been pretty ill for the past year or so. I get my mom and she has to fly north to be with her. My sister and I unpack the house. Again "this is all wrong, why am I doing this", I should be out planning a wedding, being happy and here I am unpacking my parent's house because my grandmother is sick. The month goes on and my mom is back and forth visiting my grandmother. She is doing great about the rape; her mom is taking her mind off of it. Here I am stuck at home. So Valentine's Day gets here and my dog of 14 years chokes, and quietly passes away in front of my mother and I, he also has been very sick. How much more can you take. I remember looking at my mom that night; she was crying "not you, Heine, not you". He had been there for her during her rape. He had been there for all of us while growing up. A part of the family has died. It is pouring rain outside, my dad is gone. The vet said to put him in the freezer until the next day. No way!! My brother-in-law came over at 10pm at night and dug a hole and we buried my best friend of 14 years.

That was the night the major anxiety attacks started. Not sleeping, I couldn't breathe and my life was completely out of my control. My sister is pregnant, don't want to bother her. Who do I turn to? About two weeks later I need to get out, away, needed to be a 23 year old so I decided to go visit Western Kentucky, where I graduated from college. I had a great night. I came home and mom called and she said my grandmother had passed away. That trip was horrible!! So many anxiety attacks. How does a 23 year old deal with all this when she had no-where to turn? How was my mother holding it together? I kept asking her when she was going to drop. It was so bad I could not sit in the funeral; I sat at the back and cried and cried and cried!! I couldn't wait for February to be over. I started having anxiety attacks driving to work and I don't know if you have ever had one while driving, but they do not go together!!

So now my mother has been raped and I was here for her, my grandmother has died and my dog has died. This is what I know of adult life. Post- traumatic stress disorder sets in. I fear that bad things happen at every turn and I don't think I can handle any more. The attacks get so bad I cannot go to work. I am afraid to tell my fiancé what is going on for fear he will stop loving me because I was such a basket case, my sister is pregnant and I absolutely cannot talk to my parents about how I am feeling, they have been through so much!! I decide I needed to go and talk to someone. I went to the doctor and he wants to put me on anti- anxiety pills. I didn't like this (they were not around much back then). I tried for about a week, they didn't help (I think it takes six weeks for them to kick in). So what do I do? I decide I needed to quit my job and get a less stressful one. Well it hit me that I was getting married and I could move to Atlanta, and that is what I was going to do. But what will that do for my mom? Who will be here for her? I thought I would have to get my dad to come back here and live. So I told them I was leaving and there were lots of tears, but it needed to happen. In the months to follow, we started really concentrating on the wedding and my sister had my nephew in June. The wedding happened in September and it was so beautiful. It was like a big relief for everyone; we had something good happening as well as my nephew. Whew.

The months and years would prove to be difficult to deal with. There was a lot of mental debate on my part. A lot of anxiety attacks and a lot of love. I became pregnant with my first child and life was wonderful, we were so happy. Then my second child was born, I quit my job and now I was home with a 22 month and a newborn. It was fine until it was winter (February again) and I was home with them. My best friend was on bed rest, so we couldn't get out. I was stuck again and I started getting those same feelings of being trapped in a situation I had no control over. Coupled with the pregnancy hormones and two babies, I was in hell! I should be excited and happy, but I wasn't. I felt like I didn't understand these feelings and I deserved help. I finally sought help as I was afraid for my children, what if I had a nervous breakdown and couldn't take care of them, I was scared to death. They were just babies. So finally I got some anti- anxiety medication. It has been a long road since then, but I still fight some of the anxiety battles, but working on it. Honestly if I didn't have my faith and a wonderful family, I don't know if I would have made it through. I am still on that anti-anxiety medication and will always be, but that is a small price to pay for a feeling of normalcy.

My mom has come a long way; she has always talked, talked about talking. Don't hide, don't feel ashamed. Seek help whether it is you it happened to or the support family. Don't make this your fault because it's not. Don't go through the things I have been through. You deserve help. Everyone is hurting. Don't give up on the victim, be there for them, let them talk and express their feelings, don't push them if they have problems with things like going out in public. Just be there and don't leave, but take care of yourself too. The last piece of advice I would give is keep your faith, if you don't have any, get some. You don't have to be my faith, be whatever you are. Believe that bad things do happen. But you can make those into positive experiences!! Yes, my mom is my hero. Now for much different reasons than when I was growing up. She has lived through this and now speaks to many different groups and has won awards. They are a big part of the Sexual Assault Center. She has written books and been a part of many public awareness campaigns. She is so strong, she is still my hero. Not about being the independent career woman, but through this whole thing she kept her faith, kept her family intact and is fighting every day to be normal. She still has some battles to fight, being in public, break-ins and the unexpected...but she is surviving and that is the most important thing...survival!! Do not suffer in silence!! Get help.

CHAR

Purple Mums and Sandy's Recovery

I have been following Sandy for 17 years and in these years have matured into a clinician that understands sexual assault.

I am sharing my comments on Sandy and her remarkable recovery as a therapist seeing it from the cognitive thoughts as a therapist watching a person who is in recovery and watched her make many proactive choices to heal.

Only recently did she call and inform me that they had found her stranger rapist and so another chapter begins in her recovery.

My intentions are to point out for others who are learning this field as well as others interested in these dynamics the impact on her and her family, how that has remained the same, and how it has manifested in different ways that are more of a reaction of their personalities.

Sandy's Chapter One

Let's first look at Sandy's story in the first chapter and the first impact of the sexual assault. The shock and disbelief, her taking in her surroundings, concern for her sweet, old, and beloved dog, a moment of comfort yet compassion for her in the middle of chaos. Her mind was confused and in some shock as well as her needing to free herself from her bondage by her attacker. Her first survival moments and her thoughts of the moment are trying, with difficulty, to think what to do next immediately following the leaving of the rapist. She knew she needed to see and helped free herself enough to see.

The fear set in but she forced herself to start grounding herself with the scene of where she was and what had happened. She immediately went to safety for herself and what she had to do to be safe. Her mind remained confused and was realizing she could not seem to grip what had happened. Her first thought was WHY?

The denial is a common reaction and the why did it happen?

She realizes immediately that she had survived and this so reflects the fact that most rape victims feel that they will die because the rapist will kill them. The thought is a thought and yet does not sink in. The trauma has changed her thinking around safety forever.

She forces herself to stand and yet she even has the thought that it was a dream because rape is such a surreal

Purple Mums and Sandy's Recovery

experience. She can't remember how she got where she ended up which is also a common experience for rape survivors as the body takes over to help it survive. She realizes no dream was ever this bad and forces herself to take positive action to think her way to a plan of safety first.

Her physical body has been through war and terror yet she forces her body to stand, in spite of weakness, and formulate a plan. Her mind followed. She knew that it was rape and had to be reported in spite of what he said and did to discourage her.

She chooses her next move and pushes the rapist's comments and threats out of her head, realizing that this was not her fault and she was a survivor and he must be caught. She knew she needed help immediately

She is focused on her plan to get dressed and keep the evidence intact to help the police catch the rapist. As life happens 911 was busy so instead of panicking she calls a neighbor, help, and an alternative plan. The lines were down for 911. WHY? Fortunately a neighbor was home and came over but she warned her to bring some protection with her. The neighbor took over and called for her. This connection was vital to have another human being who could do what she asked. Here was a chance to get her control back again and to have a connection to others which is much needed in the case of rape. Being seen and heard and respected is of highest value early in the trauma recovery. Humans are intuitive and reach out to others instinctively.

When she had another human there and her plan that she had focused on was in place, she let go and then the shock and the denial began to set in. There was help and safety there where she could again relax but she had no idea of the journey.

Sandy's Chapter Two

Her plans from her day had all been altered. Stopped short on that Labor Day weekend. Her life that she enjoyed had been changed. Never would she be that person before the rape as fully and as safe as she had felt at that time and at that age. Interestingly purple is the color of domestic violence and teal is the color for sexual violence. The purple mums have been her symbol of transformation to return to herself again and her new calling of helping others.

Here we can all identify with a carefree mom looking forward to returning home to celebrate her daughters' engagement. She had mapped out a plan for her weekend trip and knew what would be best for getting away when the time came. We have all been there, involved in the plan of our life when something happens to change all of this.

As she finished her plans and was ready to shift gears we can all indentify the moment when we come home into our kitchen looking for all to be as it always is. But imagine the shock and surprise of the moment at seeing an intruder in your home. What would we do? How would we react? The books all say what ever you did, you survived. The body takes over and your autonomic nervous system takes over; " Fight, Flight or Freeze". If you are a black belt in Karate you will react out of that training. If you are a former victim you might respond out of *that* conditioning and freeze. If you are neither of those you might run and try to flee as Sandy did.

This moment is the time that she knew that she might be raped or killed and there was no way out. The Anticipation phase of the recovery begins when she became aware that she was trapped, helpless, and vulnerable and could not get away and realizing that something bad was going to happen. Sheer Terror!

At this moment she knew that this was not a joke but that she was a victim of a crime and her sympathetic nervous system was on alert and the body reacted in the fight mode. She fought for as long as she could and was subdued through force and pain. She was fighting for her life. When he could not subdue her, he used a weapon. Her body kept warning her that it was about to pass out. So she survived and he knew what he was doing as he had done it before.

He had watched her as she planted mums, waiting for her to come in where he could entrap her. Opportunity and vulnerability is what all rapist look for all the time. He must have been working on one of the houses and had observed her and her schedules and planned it all out. It is difficult to defend and protect against rape with this kind of stalking occurring.

The sex was abusive and powerful to hurt and cause pain. Power and control are the rapist's weapons as well as his penis and a knife. Domination was his *Modus of Operandi*. He enjoyed hurting her and winning over her, making her less than and helpless, or so he thought. She refused to give up in her mind and that was how she empowered herself. She fought him physically and with her mind and attitude.

The ejaculation showed he was a serial rapist in his methodology as well as the rubber gloves He stalked her until he had the opportunity to get in her house and watched her from inside and then jumped her and defeated her physically, accomplished his acts, making every effort not to leave evidence leaving with a threat as they all do. He wiped up evidence or attempted to and he kept her eyes hidden as well as wore a ski mask which kept her from identifying him in court

The fear of death was very evident throughout her story. She knew the knife was close at hand and expected death to happen so that is why she submitted her body but nothing else. Survivors of rape submit in order to survive and live. He even put hand cream on her like that was some kind of kindness or was it his ritual?

She focused on family and prayer to get through the physical attack itself. And when she thought he had left, she immediately shifted to action and thinking of how to get help. She believed he could have killed her and a knife wound must really hurt, she thought. Immediately, she went to self-blame for leaving the garage door open. That helps a survivor sometimes to get control back, to blame yourself as it does make sense and is a way to function and keep going. A survivor cannot shift that fast back into the person they were before the rape.

The coping mechanisms for this kind of recovery are not built in. Each survivor must build them for herself There is no previous experience in how to heal from rape and there is no guideline. That is why getting help immediately is so important so a survivor can start telling herself the truth, not some myth that was in her head before the rape. She might think she did something to cause it or something worse.

Being vulnerable is impossible to defend against. As a human being we are vulnerable and most of us do not live from a fear-based belief system unless we have been through rape and trauma.

Sandy's Chapter Three

The arrival of the police was very nurturing to her. There was no sensationalism or sirens and for her this was comforting. Being heard and believed is so vital, the police process can help or add to a survivor's trauma. When it is not handled well, the survivor becomes a victim again. The systems that handle rape can be as traumatizing.

She was crying which is an expressed emotional release but often survivors will not shed a tear and keep saying, "I can't believe this happened to me. I can't believe I was raped." This is more of a controlled emotional style. It is a preference of the survivor. This is the beginning of the Impact or Acute stage of the rape recovery

The shock had worn off and she was safe and her feelings started flowing as she realized she had a near death experience. She kept her head down and the policeman was at her level asking her questions gently. He inquired about her physical well being and then suggested the hospital for the rape kit. He asked her if he could remove the tape. He was giving her the control and she could tell him what kind of limits she could tolerate with the tape. He gave her control and authority throughout the process being as respectful as possible.

She was beginning to be grateful for simple things and to get through the moment as best she could. They asked questions and she told them all she could but his face was covered and he did not talk much. He had worn a red shirt and this became a trigger for her whenever she saw one as well as the rubber gloves and the time of day and time on the clock.

The neighborhood had come to gather in front of her house and all were curious. She was weak and dizzy from it all and wondering where she got the strength to do all she did when he left. Adrenaline kicks in and pushes us. This is part of trauma.

She reached out to contact her husband and the police helped her with this. She even focused on being concerned for him coming home hearing, and not from her, that she had been raped. Her reporting and the way the police treated her is the exception rather than the norm.

So many women are too fearful to report immediately or if the rape was by an acquaintance they may not be sure if it is rape. They may think it was rough sex or not know that if asleep it is rape or that oral sex is rape. Who tells you this? Your mother may not even know this.

That is why there is a crisis line for sexual assault with someone who can help you figure it out if no one else does.

Sandy's Chapter Four

She was eager to leave the scene of the rape and crime. These images are ingrained in survivors' senses as these are heightened in the process of a trauma. The intrusive thoughts continue for months and are most intense in the first weeks after the attack. As they fade and are not as intense, triggers replace these thoughts and continue to remind survivors of their attack and the emotion of fear is extremely prevalent.

This begins the recovery phase called the Reconstitution or Reorganization phase because the survivors starts to build their life from the bottom up. They may appear normal but they sure don't feel normal. They have lost their former selves and have to find themselves and rebuild themselves around this event.

Next is the hospital. Another system and another possibility that the survivor will be treated with unpredictability and disrespect. They may be misunderstood, unheard, and devalued. Disbelief is very possible.

More invasiveness occurs but it has to be done to catch the rapist with evidence and to make sure the survivor has not been physically hurt internally or externally. Here are more questions and an exam that feels like a rape.

Fortunately she was treated caringly and respectfully. But there were so many questions she cannot remember. Many survivors dissociate out of everything right after the rape or they can't remember some things. This is normal for a trauma survivor. Police often question their credibility and especially if survivor had been using a substance.

Most people have no idea about what is expected or done in a rape kit. There is a protocol and nurse practitioners or medical doctors must follow this protocol. It is for collecting physical evidence for court. It is then sent to the state bureau of investigation which has a central location. Rape survivors do not have to pay for the exam.

The exam is very intrusive and detailed; swabbing the vagina and inside the mouth, pulling and combing pubic hairs, looking for semen on the body and in the mouth. A survivor has to be in shock when all of this happens and when asked, "How are you doing?" Most survivors say fine because they have no idea. It would be better to say, I am sorry this happened and to listen to the survivor and ask her to tell you what she needs and wants.

Survivors can't focus or concentrate and are often irritated. As Sandy expressed it, "I wasn't dead, but I didn't feel very alive." She did focus on the next step in the moment and made efforts to control her thinking to help herself. The "never feel the same" is a very common feeling. They feel like they are different and want desperately to be the person they were before the rape.

Counseling helps the survivor grieve and use her anger to keep pushing for revenge in a positive way. No one forgets and everyone wishes it had not happened. Often they use blame or denial to figure out how they could have kept it from happening. Many survivors wish the rapist had killed them as the recovery is so intense. Many survivors attempt or complete suicide because the recovery is so rough.

Sandy always fought back and continues to do so. Her anger has turned proactive and she is able to help others and has never ever given up because she knows that revenge is living a triumphed life and using it for good. She has dedicated the last 17 years to this process and has helped many survivors through her example.

The physical response that she went through is often the way the symptoms start with the survivor. The rape is cruelly intrusive and actually makes the survivor experience nausea and disgust at the act and never wants to repeat or think about the ugly parts ever again. Yet the rape rolls uncontrollably through their thoughts daily.

Sandy's Chapter Five

Impact on others is called secondary stress and often the family or those closest to the survivor have similar feelings and symptoms as the person who has been raped. Sandy had not talked yet to her husband, Dave, after the rape and could only imagine what he might be feeling or thinking, knowing that someone had to tell him something. Their first reunion was one of relief and emotional pain that they both felt and yet could not express in words.

We see the change that happens immediately when her once beautiful and safe house becomes a reminder of the terror that she had been through there. Many survivors leave the location where the rape happened and never return. Others have no choice but to stay. If they have a mortgage, they cannot leave.

Some ask, "Why not get back on the horse that threw you?" Where rape is concerned and survival and getting your life and self back is the issue, there is little time to suffer unnecessarily. Survivors do the best they can and make choices that are best for them at the time. The energy drain is tremendous and exhausting. The rape lives constantly in the survivor's mind and they experience it over and over again until it dies with exhaustion and it still can be called up in a second. Triggers are constant and being on guard all the time is draining .One's stress system is on constantly and the word hyper-vigilant barely encompasses the stress that must be endured and overcome. One heals but one does not forget.

Having a friend who walks with you through the process and beside you as Sandy had, is a gift and often we at the Sexual Assault Center or on the crisis line advise taking someone with you to the hospital to sit with you and be a companion. It is a difficult process. Make it as easy as possible for you. It helps to begin to build connection and human kindness and support as soon as possible. It helps to take the edge off the isolation and begins to build hope and possibility of healing. Judith Herman states, "Violence creates disconnection and healing is created through connection."

The realization and beginning adjustment came to Sandy and Dave as they watched the news and saw the rape on the news with the helicopters searching and their street and house pictured. She allowed her husband to stand between her and the callers as she is conserving the strength needed to get through these moments and did not need any more horrific reminders because they were constantly playing in her brain as intrusive thoughts.

Bathing is a special situation that most survivors have difficulty with because they can't get clean no matter how many baths they take. They are scrubbing away the disgust, shame, guilt, and nastiness of it all. She needed to feel protected so her husband stood guard right in the bathroom to help her relax enough to be invulnerable in a bath. Little things become big things in this war against violence.

She was not sleeping as the hyper arousal and hyper vigilance will not let her. Her system has been traumatized and put on alert by the terror she has been through. The body and mind keep checking to be sure it is safe. REM sleep or deep, safe sleep cannot occur for some time so chronic sleeplessness is the norm. The survivor has to be safe and the horror that they have experienced says no one is ever safe. They enter a state of new reality and vulnerability in a real sense and can't go back to the old reality that they can actually know they are safe.

Sleeplessness and insecurity haunts rape survivors and to sleep means to let go of control and they cannot. Because their minds take over in sleep and wake them up from nightmares to the reality of an unsafe world.

Often survivors change their surroundings in an attempt to trick their mind about the rape. They change their furniture around in an attempt to change what had happened so they won't repeat it in their head. It moves the triggers around. Many move out of the scene of the crime, as Sandy did, but most cannot leave their home which was their safe place. Now it becomes a constant reminder of the rape. Many survivors sleep on the sofa for months if the rape happened in their bed. They may give their bed away or redecorate by changing the bedding and colors to transform the entire room so they can tolerate it and move on with their life.

Survivors have to go on with their lives and make every effort to function and cope as best they can in spite of the horrific symptoms and reminders. Yet what is honoring what happened? Some choose to do grief work with a counselor in spite of the emotional pain and sadness and loss that comes out.

This recovery is extremely challenging. But all recovery is a way to honor the courage and the helplessness they went through in order to survive and have their life back. Without support, the returning to your former self is slow and feels impossible.

Sandy's Chapter Six

Fortunately for Sandy, all of the societal systems that interact to help rape survivors treated her with respect and dignity. This is not often the case as with many survivors they are victimized again by the helpers sent to respond to them in their emergency. This is called secondary wounding and happens over and over again for rape survivors. This process often happens when others have a misunderstanding about rape and ask ignorant questions. The survivor does not feel heard or respected and this action causes further wounding again. It can emphasize the isolation many survivors feel after a rape as no one seems to understand. Many feel that the only place where they are safe is at the rape crisis center which is where they feel connected, valued, and heard.

As we can see, Sandy was beginning to find control in the chaos after the rape as she is suspicious of everywhere and everyone as possible suspects when she stopped for lunch after leaving the police station. You see the hyper vigilance and the fear and paranoia that everyone is a rapist or everyone becomes someone who could hurt you. Many survivors wonder what is wrong with them to be so fearful but let us think about it. Before a rape you trust your environment and think it is safe. After the rape you know it is not and cannot be so everything becomes suspect.

The mind is making efforts to figure it out. The executive function of the brain wants definite answers and closure. She is thinking who could have done this? Did he watch the house and see me here at this restaurant and follow me home?

Most rapists are creatures of opportunity and vulnerability all of the time. And this part for Sandy is speculation and there is no closure there because she may never know for sure. Who? Why?

This chapter is the beginning of reality for Sandy's family. Dave is already dealing with what has happened. And is, no doubt, replaying it over and over and the intrusive thoughts of what could have happened are perhaps worse than what he has not yet learned in detail as to what actually did happen. We are all victims of what our imagination can do. But both of them are making the strong effort and stick to their plan to honor their daughter's engagement festivities. And keeping their lives going is the best choice for survivors. Stay on routine and continue your life even though that may sound insane with your mind a mess of intrusive thoughts and fear and panic are over the top. Survivors have to take control of their minds and force themselves to live their lives in spite of their minds where the craziness occurs. This takes huge courage and a strong human spirit which we all have to one degree or another.

The newspaper article and the TV news of the rape break through another layer of denial. Denial is a coping mechanism we use until we are ready to face it full on. Gradually reality breaks though the shock is wearing off there is a protection psychologically until we can accept reality as really happening.

Sandy is still in the early phase of the Rape Trauma Syndrome. The first week and months are usually the most intense and take a toll on the body and mind. There is a struggle going on between the mind and the body. The crisis reaction is a name that seems perfect, but most rape survivors want to know if they are going crazy.

Sandy needed her family support and protection and reassurance. Many survivors want someone near all the time as this helps the fear that they are not alone. She needed to feel she belonged somewhere so her family brought great comfort to her. Though she had to do the actual healing herself, her family support especially in the beginning seems to buffer her and help her to gain and build her own strength.

She wanted to keep the focus on the celebration but knew that she had to be real with her family or they would sense something was not right. So she trusted herself to know what to do. The trust is most important right after the rape. An emotionally healthy survivor always has that trust in herself and yet during the recovery it is more vital than ever because she feels she can't trust anyone. And often at times doesn't trust those closest to her because no one was there during the rape but her. So she must trust herself and what she needs and learn to ask for it.

So trusting herself gives her the beginning of a sense of safety when she has lost all external safety through the rape experience. She has the past years of strength to pull on to get through the first year of recovery.

She planned the telling of her daughters about the rape, observing herself slipping into depression. This decision to tell her daughters, knowing that the impact would be painful for her daughters, still had to be done because she needed their support. And imagine the dilemma. It happened. You must speak to them about it and bring emotional pain into their lives. Something as a parent you bend over backwards not to do to your child. You need your family to share the reality and pain. Love and support help buffer the emotional pain and stress of the awful ordeal. Those with support early do better and recover more quickly.

The breaking of the bubble of security and safety! A happy family where tragedy breaks in! It happened to mom, so it can happen to us. The shock and the grief! Each person close to the survivor experiences her/his own grief, loss, and mourning.

Mother is the protector and now she had to break that code. But being real is always best. I am sure it felt like role reversal but they are part of the family unit and are affected. Secondary victims often have the same set of symptoms that rape survivors have. They hear and see her reactions and know that she has survived trauma.

The night of family bonding/celebration turned into terror because of Sandy's screaming from her nightmares and waking them up to the shock of the tragedy and reality of her symptoms. As Eve Ensler says, "One is slammed dunked into a new reality". Sleep becomes a luxury that will not occur as automatically as before. The after rape or new reality was here with a vengeance. And since her daughters were there spending the night with them in the hotel, they knew this was serious and not going to go away immediately. Dave also realized that he could not cope alone and needed professional help.

Fortunately he reached out for help immediately and found it. This help is the safe harbor. Someone willing to be there now, to hear you—to be your guide and coach. A therapist trained in the field to help understand it all.

Recovery saps the survivor's strength as it takes huge psychic energy to get through the day much less the healing. But without a guide there is no time line, no encourager, no way of knowing how you are doing through the recovery.

Everyone needs a check point to keep their hope high and to be the voice that says, "You can survive this and you will be fine. It just takes time and there is plenty of time."

Most survivors want to push it or get through it fast. Just like society, they want to get over it and go on with their life. It's like a broken bone. It doesn't heal overnight. You are worthy of time and honor. And this is what it has taken.

Gaining one's control back is seen as Sandy makes decisions about who to tell and why. This is a most important part of honoring herself as she desires. It is her story and her information and her decision. She protected herself, knowing what she needed and she used her skills wisely to take care of herself.

Honoring oneself is just this: self care which is self love, compassion, and empathy for self. At this time, many survivors internalize the denigration that society places on rape survivors for being raped. Self-love is important and a most crucial step, because this becomes the base on which the survivor builds outward and upward.

Sandy's Chapter Seven

In this chapter there is more support for Sandy. This is always great, but the survivor must monitor her needs. The sensitivity to noise and crowds is part of the hyper arousal which occurred intensely during the rape and was part of the body's automatic "fight, flight, freeze" stress response.

But the withdrawal from the impact of the adrenaline doesn't happen overnight. The survivors have to limit the impact of the triggers by structuring their time with others and time alone, a balance that seems weird at times because they haven't had to do this before. We can see Sandy doing it with her sister's visit of connection and then a limit, where she needed down time and she identified her need for "strength and stability" —a need which she gave to herself without judgment.

Knowing what you need and asking for it is healthy and emotionally mature, not selfish especially when healing. You must put youself and your needs first.

Sandy relives her experience of the rape for the first time. This is often a most anxious and fearful time. Therefore crucial for her and therapist.

Fortunately for Sandy she received immediate attention and due to her recent rape an immediate appointment for therapy.

Research has suggested immediate intervention helps with recovery, breaks the cognitions and beliefs that may be faulty. Each survivor brings her/his history of experience and what she has learned. Therapy is concentrated immediately on breaking the myths our culture holds about rape.

Knowing how and where to get knowledgeable help is crucial. The women's movement in the 70's opened the way for survivors to begin speaking their truths about the reality of sexual assault as children and in their marriages and relationships. These stories raised consciousness about the need for healing, so Rape Crisis Centers sprang up all over the country and have grown into efficient clinical therapy centers specializing in the impact of sexual assault and offering help to the family and children.

One in 4 girls and 1 in 6 boys will be sexually abused by the time they are 18. One in 4 women will be raped in their lifetime. Finding help is very possible with internet resources.

Resurrection After Rape by Matt Atkison LCSW is available online at resurrectionafterrape.org. There is a guide to finding a competent knowledgeable rape counselor and information and help for family members who need to know how to support you through this recovery. Boyfriends, fathers, and others have distorted beliefs about rape and once they read the facts they usually come on board as advocates and helpers.

Give yourself the gift of a helper and coach. You would never dream of not going to the doctor for illness or a broken leg. This is trauma; an out-of-the-ordinary experience, a near death experience. It has changed you. Your traumatized self needs attention. You want your old self back, someone who can listen non-judgmentally and allow you to come back to you. It's homecoming, a return to you. It's too lonely to do it by yourself.

Sandy's Chapter Eight

Sandy began a new life, living at the hotel with her daughter. Dave had a new life commuting. She spoke freely about her rape to her friends. She allowed herself this freedom to trust them so that they could understand.

Protecting others uses a lot of energy that one needs to get through the day so she allowed others to be there for her. She refused to feel shame as she put all responsibility where it should go—on the rapist It's all his doing so the blame goes to him.

She describes her social outing and how a survivor can feel she can't depend on herself as rape recovery has a mind and life of its own.

She is in a social situation and is fine one minute and the next she is not, out of the blue "all was not fine." The noise of the chatter may have been a trigger and she dropped her glass. The chatter made her feel unsafe where she couldn't hear so she reacted from danger. It helped facilitate her telling everyone who could support her.

Many survivors fear judgment and secondary wounding due to many people's denial, doubting, ignorant cruelty, generalizations, discounting, and blaming the victim attitude. They often feel they are losing it or going crazy because of the physical and emotional reactions of hyper arousal that is triggered throughout recovery.

In the early acute stages of weeks to months, the reactions and/or symptoms are more intense and slowly and individually depending on each ones unique situation, become less intense as one moves away from the date of the rape. It has been called the disorganization phase because it feels this way and looks this way.

Your life is put on hold to heal and it has a plan all its own. In some ways survivors feel frustrated with its unpredictability and lack of structure and accountability.

I remember Sandy telling me about being in the grocery and looking over the meat for ideas for dinner. A man made a comment to her and she overreacted as it stimulated her startle response. She said she had to go home right then—leave her shopping cart and leave. This was result of a trigger that caused a release of adrenaline and she couldn't calm down so she went home for the day.

Many survivors feel this is a sign of craziness when in reality it is your body reacting to protect you— consequences common to both hyper arousal and numbing (Matsakis P. 104 *Trust after Trauma*).

Sandy's Chapter Nine

Speaking to others when ready offers a way of empowering the survivors. It is also a way of educating others about recovery and why rape survivors heal, survive and thrive. The amount of energy it takes is huge to just get through the day. Eventually you hit the worst phase in recovery which is the long term or chronic phase of healing where the symptoms are less intense and less frequent and a rebuilding of the survivor's life begins. This has been called the Reorganizational phase of healing where the survivor begins to take back her life for him/herself and rebuilds it into an integrated whole. The survivor remembers and talks about the rape without shame or blame except where blame should go—on the rapist, and sees self with self compassion and love. She accepts this event as a part of life's experiences and integrates safety, structure, and control back into her life.

The best revenge for rape is living a full life that is worth living. Sandy made her decision to write and talk about it to help others. She turned her tragedy into courage and strength with empathy, compassion and hope for others. Education and prevention are the keys to success around rape. Breaking the silence takes courage and inner strength. It offers channeling your anger and rage into a proactive activity to offer help and perspective to others.

Sandy gained strength, honor, structure and empowerment with new confidence. Her belief in God—

something outside of herself, helped her to find meaning in the trauma and suffering. This gives the survivor the power over the rapist and the empowerment of the true self. Taking purple mums as a symbol of victory over defeat is her example.

Sandy's Chapter Ten

Getting back to routine, making long term decisions, and not feeling totally healed are part of an ongoing decision of new life changes. Rape survivors go through fear of being alone. They are not ready to stay alone and other life events keep occurring. They have to use energy to balance their recovery with self-care and continue to build their new life after rape.

Sandy's mother's illness, her husband's changes at work, and her need to travel to Iowa to be with her mother are examples of her life continuing. Her mom's illness created new challenges but these changes also meant new strengths and building for her through these decisions and life experiences.

She again reveals her rape to an aunt but outlines her boundaries and requests that she not tell her mom. She acted so beautifully and instinctively protective of herself and others which gave her control of her information and let her speak her truths. She needed and wanted to emphasize her power over information and her readiness to speak her truth.

The support that Dave and Sandy received from the company he worked for shows the wonderful support that community and society can offer when informed and educated.

The losses of life do not stop when rape recovery is in process. Most survivors know better how to negotiate these life losses of parents and animals since they know how to grieve and honor themselves in this healing. Sandy realized she had to become active in the fight against violence. Through her life experiences and healing, she made a commitment to be a voice for survivors, a rallying call to take back your life. Taking it back for herself she became and is a role model for us all. She did not let her affluence protect her. She used it as a platform to speak and to empower all survivors.

Sandy's Chapter Eleven

Sandy comments on the return to work in travel, her long term triggers, and how she handles them and her new mature person who developed past the rape recovery. She integrated her experiences into a wholeness that is real, intimate and awesome. She does not turn bitter and alone with only anger as power but pushes for social change and uses her anger and rage proactively to speak and counts her blessings each day.

Dave's Chapter - Men and Rape

Dave, as the husband and significant other, is impacted by symptoms and his style of relating and discussing the impact is straight forward and cognitively focused.

The impact and symptoms are seen in his telling his side of the story focused on facts. Being taught to be the protector, men often feel an anger that is directed correctly toward the rapist and on the facts. While dealing with what is needed, they often watch their loved one suffer and feel helpless in relieving the suffering. They may feel helpless in their inability to protect and need the support of therapy to deal with their side of the impact.

Their anger can be misdirected at the survivor. But most men, after education about rape place the anger on the rapist.

The frustration and depression cover up their inability to actually make more of an impact on the survivor and the process toward healing. But in actuality they can be great sources of security and help by just allowing her to lean on them or just be with them in the intimacy of the moment of whatever state she is in.

Our society has assigned men to feel they can FIX problems and situations. Their business trained them to be problem solvers and rewards them for this. But rape recovery has to be a problem that the survivor fixes and works out.

Men can get help from counselors, face their own frustrations and stay for support. It will pass into an easier stage and your relationship will grow if you are willing. It takes patience but the pay off will come through in time.

Dave was away when Sandy was sexually assaulted and this must have been difficult for him and her, yet he made his way back as soon as he could and his business supported him throughout with calling—giving him time and support.

The goodness came. Most rape victims (85%) submit because they freeze in terror. All believe they will die when it is over. But whatever you do, you survived and this means you did the right thing! Dave must have felt relieved and yet intrusive thoughts probably started then—a form of SHOCK to hear his wife had been raped and he was not there.

He saw the chaos happening: getting home seeing the neighborhood in disarray, must have reflected a kind of bewilderment and lost feelings of things not being right and being the lead story on the news must have felt surreal.

His lack of clarity is normal in trauma. Your brain can't believe it and must replay it over and over until accepted. Your memory doesn't perform well when stressed by trauma.

Often survivors are in such shock that it is difficult to think, often they can't remember details. Women usually are better at describing details of the attacker. Memories can come back especially in a drugged rape. This often takes weeks and months before the whole picture returns and many get nothing but a few pieces.

Recovery from rape is just like anything in that it is difficult to predict since there are so many variables. Each survivor can only speak of their individual experience. And many of these are similar but never just alike. Our individuality is part of our specialness.

With constant support from his business, Dave put his attention on his wife and being with her throughout whatever the ordeal entailed. He managed all the nuts and bolts so Sandy could be protected now that he was home.

He found a place of safety and refuge for them. He went back to Indiana to get the house ready to sell. Sandy knew she could not and would not return and fortunately she didn't have to.

Dave reviewed the processes of law enforcement bringing in the FBI and doing everything to cooperate.

His suspicions would be normal. They both had normal thinking about who the rapist was and where is he and how and why and what? All the open questions we are left with after trauma.

Activities may have helped Dave to get through it and focus in the moment, which often is the best you can do—just get through it, survive it, and function each day. Then review and sit with the uncertainty.

His depression was obvious to me and he spent a couple of sessions with me in therapy. Seeing his helplessness as depression was very real and normal. Sitting with this depression is difficult even for a therapist but it helps to normalize and encourage survivors and partners through it.

His safety was taken away, too. Survivors and others realize anything can happen anytime to anyone. No one is protected. We have to make peace with the unjust, unsafe world and not live in fear. We owe it to ourselves to live free and empowered. It can be done!

The traveling got to be exhausting and not a lifestyle to adopt. He eventually changes this but talked about his symptoms of intrusive thoughts (thoughts focus on Sandy and what she is going through or imagine her state of mind). Sleeplessness is a hallmark of trauma—nighttime is not as safe so survivors vamp up the hyper arousal and fear at night. With the loss of safety, of course, sleep is impossible. Adrenaline won't let you. Safety is an illusion and after rape you know it.

Dave's mind was so active he couldn't sleep. This is survival. Once hyped the mind won't let go. We have to bore it to death by focused exercises to sleep. Dave's survival was work. Travel, selling house, dealing with nuts and bolts, cleaning, sorting, reading, distracting and survival. He was trying to bring order and structure back to their life.

After finally selling the house, they could purchase their home in Tennessee which may have represented a new form of safety.

Sandy wanted an open floor plan so she could see it all and feel safe. Her needs had changed. Give yourself what you need if you can. Dave continued to be the rock to provide, to work, and support Sandy's recovery.

Dave remembers all the support, reduced rates and community care and concern that helped the family. Feeling loved and appreciated helps them heal. You decide you have to move in and make changes and you do.

Being settled at home in Nashville, Dave had to make do on the road. Seeing his description of where he lived was depressing, but he was on remote or robot. Just one foot in front of the other and get through it.

Steady strengthened movement found a new life without the trauma with new structure and new safety and life began to look normal again!

Dreading to return to Chicago is a burnout or secondary stress reaction. Wanting the house to be sold and finished with the back and forth is avoidance which can prolong PTSD but with the support from the company and the settling of expenses, this offers Dave a new hope and getting some kind of normal was coming into reality.

Dave does a great job in stating his newly formed philosophy that developed because of the trauma. This attitude toward change and letting oneself see value and gain in tragedy helps honor the gains as well as grieve the losses. This helps balance the change.

If you learn and grow and see the abundance in it then you can move on. But this takes time. He listened to counsel and realized how he had coped and yet allowed himself to become more empathetic and it even served him to help others he knew or ran into through business.

By being open to emotional pain we allow our own strength through weakness to come forth. This takes courage and is tinged with fear but the payoff is huge.

Dave and Sandy began to give back when ready. They helped our Center in the way that best suited their talents and became a blessing through the Center for hundreds and thousands of people over the years. Pass it on is what they did and are still doing. He found, as many do, that their vulnerability is built into a strength that endures into positive attitude toward others and self.

In realizing the silver lining, he lists all the positive outcomes that they found through help that others gave them. They begin to realize they were being blessed each time they gave.

We all have a choice as to our attitude. It takes just as much energy to be positive as negative. By choosing the good, we are victorious because we pass on our strengths. Only through giving does more good happen.

Evil cannot prevail in the darkness for the light is too strong.

Laura's Chapter

Laura opens with a great statement about her preference for dealing with emotions. This is her style. We all have the preferred way we like to function.

But take a moment to think how you would have handled your rock going through this as you helplessly stood by.

People refuse, through denial, the rape of my mom can happen. No—anyone but not her. The same questions of fears and doubts pop and intrude."

To see it in newsprint on the front page. NO—This can't be real. I will not let it be real. But seeing it day and night and yet seeing her heal and be strong certainly sends an encouraging message to all daughters. She is a rock and she refused to give in or let it change her.

Laura fills us in on the closeness or intimacy of the family and the childhood of security which built a strong base of love and fun memories of protection and safety up to this day. Something we all can identify with.

She gives us details on loving parents honoring each child with support, teachings, acceptance and love. Mom was there whenever she was needed. Laura also gives the reality and strength she saw in her parents' relationship.

Seeing her father cry added to the emotional pain of her experience. Here her two rocks were cracking she feared. Hearing her mom scream, one can only imagine the deep sense of loss, grief and emotional pain that hit Laura.

Describing it as the worst night of her life gives us a glimpse of what she felt.

She describes how she managed to survive and a huge appreciation and admiration for her sister who was at mom's side through most of the intense time. Since she was pregnant with her son and had a daughter, she was supportive as much as she could.

We are each blessed with strengths and these are hugely tested during difficult times. We must remember we are all doing the best we can and if a bubble can allow space, this honors the process.

The bubble was a protection for Laura. It's a good thing not a bad one. We all have limits and we must respect ourselves and where we are.

Laura sees strength in her mom and Amy but she too came to support the center and all survivors through her support of others, especially her mom. We all have a purpose and must follow that path which is our truth.

Amy's Chapter

Amy begins with a picture of the before. The calm and the normal before the shock of reality. The moment our lives would never be the same. Ton of bricks is a great metaphor for the shock, like a tornado. Here and gone before you know it.

You can't catch your breath. POW—Crisis, shock, disbelief—Wait not our mom—No Wait—confusion. This refers to the questions, the chaos, the imbalance and the shock. Explain. Help me see this clearly. How on earth? Why us? Why me? No answers. These are what all survivors search for.

The whole family is victimized and copes as best they can with their part of the story.

The helplessness and pain, grief and loss is clearly demonstrated in Amy's account—and not knowing what to do. All victims are survivors. All need counseling and help.

The confusion and helplessness set in. What do we do, how do we cope? She sees her mother's change right before her eyes and helplessly watches. She sees the traumatized self and does not know what to do.

Amy saw her mother falling apart but recovering. She saw the re-experiencing of the trauma through nightmares and triggers, the avoidance of reminders of the rape. But they were everywhere especially in her mind. She avoided going out to avoid triggers, but they were constantly in her mind. The hyper arousal, panic, emotions, depression, fear of others (especially behind her) surprised her.

Amy's description of quietly going crazy is what many survivors feel and need constant reassurance that they are not losing it but coping the best they can.

Amy provided companionship and kept her mom's fear down when it came to not staying alone with father traveling. It takes the second stage of recovery to kick in before being alone happens and only a little bit at a time.

By being extremely nurturing, caring, and supportive of your traumatized self, she will come back in time. No extremes—slow and steady wins the race.

Inspecting the apartment is a routine all survivors go through. Having walked into your safe home and finding it unsafe you have to search the area everyday—check the closets and locks. It is normal and healthy. Just have to. Let yourself do whatever and don't care what anyone thinks or says. They haven't been through what you have so they can't know.

Being safe and staying safe becomes a full time job and drains you. Your use of energy in recovery is exhausting but you can't get to sleep, stay asleep, or be asleep for long without a nightmare and you are awake.

This is part of processing through recovery until integration happens and into your lifestyle. You do whatever you do and know it has to be done—deadbolts—check and recheck, double check doors—alarms and more.

Amy observes her mother making every effort to put her life back together to recapture what had worked before to help distract herself from her symptoms that seemed more like torture but the end does come. But when?

All survivors say, how long? In your time—when? When it's over—you'll know. Trust the process. I'm tired of fighting. Then quit fighting, rest, distract. It will be there tomorrow. Put the armor down for the day. When is it over? When it's over, you will know I say: There is plenty of time. You will heal. Just believe.

Believe in something outside yourself. Sandy's intentions were to hold the light in the darkness by going to church—something she could do that symbolized hope and healing. Choosing to believe and hope gives us strength and comfort.

The symptoms began to show on Amy. Tears of grief, fear and sleeplessness are her own reactions. It began to shut her down and she needed to take care of herself. Her reaction was that it is not fair. This is out of order as she is supposed to take care of me. The anger at her mom being stolen from her during this celebration wedding dress time was not working for her.

She realized how the whole family needed counseling and yet being in it you are caught unaware in the craziness of it.

Amy again was caught up in a process with no one there to help her. She had no idea about what was happening but her emotions were a signal for her to take care of herself.

With all of the new grief and strategies, it was a crazy merry go round and she couldn't stop and had no brakes or controls. Things just kept happening. Life keeps going.

She realizes her predicament and she was between a rock and a hard place. Catch 22.

Going to Atlanta probably saved her. But without adequate counseling the recovery she needed, but had to put off due to life events, came back to bite and she began to help herself.

Medicine helps many people and many people need it during the recovery because you need spikes when crossing a glacier. Right? And this recovery for anyone is a glacier. We all react differently, have different levels of functioning so we must decide. If it helps, use it. If not—don't. Take care of you now. As Amy says "it's a small price for feeling normal".

Keep your faith and do not suffer. Help is right here.

Sandy's Final Chapter

The final chapter of the book shows the transformation from tragedy to triumph. It helps encourage, inspire and help others to believe in the possibility of life after rape.

Sandy continues to allow herself to notice positive gains which often are related to her safety and a deeper awareness which is an important gain personally. A stronger self. A more mature self.

She keeps the triggers she wants and yet understands their origins as not fear related but safety related. This is her choice to empower herself with her decisions.

The ultimate beauty and strength is her honoring of her own recovery. She has always loved purple and then the rape turned that image into a symbol of fear and loss. Her recovery turned it back into a belief in herself and a celebration of her recovery of her life. A pride and belief in her values.

Her example offers hope to all!

www.ingramcontent.com/pod-product-compliance
Lightning Source LLC
Chambersburg PA
CBHW030330080526
44584CB00012B/795